# GATE TO CÆSAR

BY

## WILLIAM C. COLLAR, A.M.
HEAD MASTER ROXBURY LATIN SCHOOL

GINN & COMPANY

BOSTON · NEW YORK · CHICAGO · LONDON

The Athenæum Press

GINN & COMPANY · PRO-
PRIETORS · BOSTON · U.S.A.

# PREFACE.

THE recent discovery of a work of Aristotle has inter-
ested and delighted the whole learned world; but one may
venture to say that if, instead, a book had been found
written in the best period of the Latin language for the
amusement or instruction of youth, by some Roman De
Foe, or Goldsmith, or Lamb, or Burnett, there would be ten
times the reason for rejoicing. Unhappily there is no
likelihood that we shall ever congratulate ourselves on
such a "find," for probably no such work ever existed.
What a misfortune that it did not occur to Cicero to divert
himself in some leisure hour by writing a story for Roman
youth! Millions of boys and girls in these later ages would
have had good reason to bless his name. Cæsar could have
done it; but to him, too, the gods denied such an inspiration,
and we must suffer for it. Seeing that he had composed a
treatise on Latin Grammar, one almost wonders that a mind
so original and fertile should not have conceived the idea
of adapting his Gallic War, or some part of it, to the
powers and comprehension of youth. What measureless
gratitude would he not have won from unborn generations
of schoolmasters, who have now to struggle desperately and
often unavailingly to make clear to their pupils the meaning
of his intricate periods, and untwist the strands of his
knotty syntax!

Cæsar is a difficult author. Some parts of his Gallic War are as hard, or nearly as hard, as any prose Latin that has come down to us. Yet it has somehow strangely enough become the fashion to read that work first in a Latin course. My own conviction is that for young learners a year's reading in easier Latin is not too much before taking up the less difficult books of the Gallic War. Even then the transition to Cæsar comes with something of a shock; for the learner is soon and often brought face to face with sentences that seem to him of most bewildering intricacy, however they may, as commentators sometimes remark, beautifully illustrate most important principles of Latin order and construction. There is a sentence in the second book, by no means the most difficult one to be found, that extends through eighteen lines, — that is, something more than half a page, — containing twenty-one distinct ideas, and having the verb separated from its subject by ninety-four words.

I know no more disheartening task than that of undertaking to carry a class unprepared in age and knowledge of the language through Cæsar's Gallic War. Yet it is precisely this disheartening task that thousands of teachers are set to do, or set themselves to do, every year. The results are often dismal enough. Teachers are blamed, they blame themselves, they blame their pupils. Pupils may sometimes be stupid, teachers may lack knowledge of the language and the subject, but the fault may also lie wholly with the author or with the Latin language itself; if with the latter, there is no help. Latin, it must be confessed, is an exceedingly difficult language to learn. All the more reason then why, in attacking it, every unnecessary obstacle should be removed. We should make our approaches with caution and skill; we should take it, if possible, *aperto latere*. We should not begin with a difficult work; or if, in the dearth of Latin suited to the juvenile mind, this is deemed unavoidable, common sense suggests the query, *why not remove provisionally* [1] *from the text those more intricate parts that discourage the learner and bar the way of progress?*

Cæsar knew how to write his own language well; but he wrote for men, he wrote with compression and in haste, and there are passages in his works that are tough reading for a good Latin scholar. It is the fashion to praise Cæsar's lucidity; but brevity and haste are not conducive to lucidity.

> "Ther nys no werkman, what so ever he be,
> That may bothe werke wel, and hastily.
> This wol be doon at leyser parfitly."

For my part I confess that I sometimes find him obscure. Moreover, when I am in doubt as to his meaning and appeal to the commentators, I find that they generally disagree and sometimes quarrel about the sense. Therefore to put young learners to reading Cæsar as his text stands, bristling with difficulties, before they have acquired anything more than a meagre vocabulary and gained a modicum of insight by some practice in reading easier Latin, is to set them at a task harder than that which Pharaoh set the Israelites.

I am of the opinion that, even when a fair working vocabulary has been acquired through some previous reading, there is no book of the Gallic War that does not require a certain degree of simplification to bring it to the level of the powers of young boys and girls. It is this conviction born of long observation of the vexation of spirit, discouragement, and waste of time by pupils in wrestling with difficulties that

---

[1] It is presumed that the learner will subsequently read the complete text.

inevitably floor them, that has prompted me to put my
hand to this work, which, slight as it may seem, has cost me
the leisure of many months. But I shall feel repaid ten-
fold, if, through this little book, boys and girls are enabled
to read Cæsar with less waste of time, more easily, with
fresher interest, and added sense of power; if, in other
words, it proves in reality what it is in name, a Gate to
Cæsar.

A few words will be sufficient to explain the principle on
which I have simplified Cæsar's text, the amount of excision,
and the degree of change. It would have been a compara-
tively easy task to simplify the text by the mere process
of omission, never deviating from the *ipsissima verba* of the
author by so much as the change of a mode or tense. One
could do this and still string together the *disjecta membra*
of the text into something like a connected narrative. But
that would be to preserve the integrity of the words at the
expense of everything else, — inner relation, structure, style,
spirit. Or the simplification might be effected by a virtual
rewriting of the text, by amplification rather than suppres-
sion, coupled with changes in the collocation of words,
where the arrangement seemed to obscure the meaning and
perplex the learner.

My purpose and plan differed essentially from both these
methods. My aim has been, first, to keep the narrative in-
tact; second, to retain as much of the text as was consistent
with the effort to disburden it of its greater difficulties;
third, to make the fewest practicable changes in what was
retained, save the modification of some verb forms, and
the occasional rendering of indirect into direct discourse;
fourth, very rarely to change the position of a word;
finally, never to insert a word, except now and then

to supply a form plainly understood, or to introduce some connective, like *et, tum, itaque, autem, ergo, postremo.*

As to the amount of excision, I find that I have omitted almost exactly one-fifth of Cæsar's text.

If the beginner in Cæsar reads the simplified text and concurrently turns the Exercises into Latin, laying firm hold of the grammatical principles selected for illustration, I believe he will find the remaining difficulties of the original text not beyond his scope. I should even hope that he would then read with something of the joy of conscious power. If the reading of the texts and the writing of the Exercises should require more time than is usually spent on the second book of Cæsar, which, however, I doubt, I believe subsequent progress would still be rapid and satisfactory enough to amount to a net gain and saving of time.

It has seemed best to mark long vowels, except the vowels of final syllables and of monosyllables, the rules for which can be readily learned. I have, however, marked a few monosyllables, as a constant reminder to teachers who find their old pronunciation clinging to certain words. We used to say *hĭs, sĭc, nŏn, quĭn, hŏc.* These words, therefore, I have marked. On the other hand, one is in no danger of saying *dĕ, hĭ, sĭ, prŏ,* for old habit would not mislead.

I take pleasure in acknowledging my obligations to Mr. Alfred G. Rolfe for several useful criticisms, and to Miss Caroline Ober Stone for valuable corrections and for carefully reading the proof-sheets as far as the vocabularies. To Mr. Clarence W. Gleason I am specially indebted. But for his timely and generous aid in preparing both vocabularies, the publication of this book must have been very considerably delayed.

WILLIAM C. COLLAR.

SEACONNET. July 25, 1891.

# CONTENTS.

———◆◇◆———

ix

# NOTE ON THE USE OF THE BOOK.

The Simplified Text and the Exercises based upon it are of the first importance. The *viva voce* translation of the Exercises, followed by the writing of them, will illustrate and help to implant in the memory the most important principles of syntax met with in the text. Let the teacher insist upon thorough work here, and he may safely omit other syntactical instruction.

But little power of reading Latin can be gained without making the acquisition of a working vocabulary a distinct object. The Latin synonyms and the Etymological Vocabulary may be made useful agents to that end. If the words added to each chapter are read aloud, reviewed, and compared where backward references are made, the learner will acquire a useful stock of synonyms easily, naturally, and with small expenditure of time.

It is often easier to retain in mind a number of words, grouped according to some principle of similarity or contrast, than a single word with nothing to hook it to the memory. For this reason it is recommended that the Etymological Vocabulary be often pressed into the service. Suppose, for example, the word *conspectus* occurs in the lesson. If the teacher will turn to page 138 and have the ten words read out under the root SPEC, he will multiply several times the chances that this particular word will be remembered on its next occurrence. He will have done much more. He will have increased the chances that nine other words will be lodged in the memory; and to each one a fresh interest will be added by its being seen in relation, not as an isolated, and therefore barren, fact.

The first vocabulary may be used for comparing in the text the different meanings and uses of the same word. It is through such comparisons that one gets at the heart and spirit of the language, while cultivating at the same time a mental habit of great value.

Having read the Simplified Text, the learner should be well equipped for wrestling with the difficulties that remain in the unchanged text, for he is already familiar with the thought and the language. Comparison of the two texts by the teacher, so far as time permits, may now be made to illustrate important principles, as of indirect discourse, which are here and there discussed in the notes.

# CÆSAR'S GALLIC WAR

## Book II.

### B.C. 57; A.U.C. 697.

—◆◆—

### THE BELGIAN LEAGUE DEFEATED.

Simplified Text.

*The Belgæ form a league against the Romans.*

**1.** Cum esset Caesar in citeriōre Gallia, crēbrī ad eum rūmōres adferēbantur. Litteris item Labiēni certior fiē-bat omnēs Belgas contrā populum Rōmānum coniūrāre obsidēsque intèr sē dare. Coniūrandi hae erant causae; prīmum verēbantur ne ad se exercitus noster addūcerē- 5 tur; deinde ab nōnnūllis Gallis sollicitābantur. Hi Ger-mānos diūtius in Gallia versāri nōluerant et populi Rōmāni exercitum hiemāre atque inveterāscere in Gallia moleste ferēbant. Nōnnūlli mōbilitāte et levitāte animi novis imperiīs studēbant. Ab nōnnūllis etiam sollicitābantur, 10 quod in Gallia a potentiōribus atque iis qui ad condū-cendos homines facultātes habēbant, vulgo rēgna occupā-bantur; qui minus facile eam rem imperio nostro cōnsequi poterant.

| | |
|---|---|
| **crēber,** *frequens.* | **versor:** *maneo, sum.* |
| **vereor,** *timeo.* | **moleste,** *graviter.* |
| **deinde,** *tum.* | **studeo,** *cupio.* |

1

*Cæsar levies two legions and marches against them.*

**2.** Hīs nūntiīs litterīsque commōtus est Caesar. Duas
legiōnes in citeriōre Gallia novas cōnscrīpsit. In interiōrem Galliam quī hās legiōnes dēdūceret Q. Pedium
lēgātum mīsit. Ipse, cum prīmum pābulī cōpia esse
5 inciperet, ad exercitum vēnit. Senones fīnitimī Belgīs
erant. Ea quae apud Belgas geruntur cōgnōscunt Caesa-
remque de hīs rēbus certiōrem faciunt. Hi cōnstanter
omnes nūntiāvērunt manus cōgī, exercitum in ūnum locum
condūci. Tum vēro nōn dubitāvit Caesar quīn ad eos
10 proficīscerētur. Itaque castra movet diēbusque circiter
quīndecim ad fīnes Belgārum pervenit.

nūntius, *rūmor.*             cōgo, *conligo.*
fīnitimus : *vīcīnus, propīnquus.*   condūco, *conligo.*
gero: *ago, facio.*             pervenio, *accēdo.*

*The Remi at once show the white feather.*

**3.** Eo de imprōvīso celeriterque vēnit Caesar. Rēmi
ad eum lēgātos Iccium et Andocumborium mīsērunt, quī
dīxērunt se omnia in fidem atque in potestātem populī
Rōmānī permittere. "Rēmi neque cum Belgīs reliquīs
5 cōnsēnsērunt neque contra populum Rōmānum coniūrā-
vērunt. Parātī sunt obsides dare et Caesaris imperāta
facere et eum oppidis recipere et frūmento cēterīsque rēbus
iuvāre. Reliqui omnes Belgae in armīs sunt. Germānī,
quī cis Rhēnum incolunt, sēse cum hīs coniūnxērunt.
10 Tantus est eōrum omnium furor ut ne Suessiōnes quidem
dēterrēre possint Rēmi. Suessiōnes frātres Rēmōrum cōn-
sanguineīque sunt eōdemque iūre et īsdem lēgibus ūtuntur.
Ūnum imperium ūnumque magistrātum cum iis habent."

de imprōvīso: *subito, repente.*   cōnsentio : *coniūro, me coniungo.*
permitto, *dēdo.*              dēterreo, *dissuādeo.*

*Cæsar learns the number of the enemy's forces.*

4. Cum ab hīs quaereret quae cīvitātes quantaeque in armis essent et quid in bello possent, sīc reperiēbat: plērīque Belgae sunt orti ab Germānis Rhēnumque antīquitus trāducti ibi cōnsēdērunt, Gallōsque qui ea loca incolēbant expulērunt. Sōli fuerunt qui Teutonos Cim- 5 brōsque intra fīnes suōs ingredi prohibuērunt. Qua ex re fīēbat ut māgnam sibi auctōritātem māgnōsque spīritus in re mīlitāri sūmerent. De numero eōrum omnia se habēre explōrāta Rēmi dīcēbant. Quantam quisque multitūdinem in commūni Belgārum concilio ad id bellum pol- 10 licitus esset cōgnōverant. Plūrimum inter eos Bellovaci et virtūte et auctōritāte et hominum numero valēbant. Hi poterant cōnficere armāta mīlia centum; polliciti sunt ex eo numero ēlecta sexāginta tōtīusque belli imperium sibi postulāvant. Suessiōnes Rēmōrum erant fīnitimi; 15 lātissimos ferācissimōsque agros possidēbant. Apud eos fuit rēx nostra etiam memoria Divitiacus, tōtīus Galliae potentīssimus, qui cum māgnae partis hārum regiōnum tum etiam Britanniae imperium obtinuit. Nunc erat rēx Galba; ad hunc propter iūstitiam prūdentiamque suam 20 belli summa dēlāta est.

| | |
|---|---|
| quaero, *interrogo.* | explōro, *cōgnōsco.* |
| reperio, *cōgnōsco.* | valeo, *possum.* |
| orior, *nāscor.* | cōnficio, *comparo.* |
| cōnsīdo, *me colloco.* | ferax, *fertilis.* |
| spīritus: *adrogantia, animī.* | summa: *cūra, imperium.* |

*He takes hostages from the Remi and crosses the Axona.*

5. Caesar omnem senātum ad se convenīre prīncipumque līberos obsides ad se addūci iūssit. Quae omnia ab hīs dīligenter ad diem facta sunt. Ipse Divitiacum Aeduum

māgno opere cohortātus est. Rei pūblicae interest manus
5 hostium distinēri, ne cum tanta multitūdine ūno tempore
cōnflīgendum sit. Id fieri potest, si suas cōpias Aedui
in fīnes Bellovacōrum intrōdūxerint et eōrum agros popu-
lāri coeperint. Hīs mandātis eum ab se dīmittit. Postea
Caesar omnes Belgārum cōpias in ūnum locum coāctas
10 ad se venīre vīdit neque iam longe abesse. Hōc ab iis
quōs mīserat explōrātōribus et ab Rēmis cōgnōvit. Tum
flūmen Axonam exercitum trādūcere mātūrāvit atque ibi
castra posuit. Quae res latus ūnum castrōrum rīpis flūminis mūniēbat et post eum quae essent tūta ab hostibus
15 reddēbat. Commeātus etiam ab Rēmis reliquīsque cīvitātibus sine perīculo portāri poterant. In eo flūmine pōns
erat. Ibi praesidium pōnit et in altera parte flūminis
Q. Titurium Sabīnum lēgātum cum sex cohortibus relī-
quit; castra in altitūdinem pedum XII vāllo fossāque
20 duodēvīginti pedum mūnīre iubet.

| | |
|---|---|
| iubeo, *impero*. | populor, *vāsto*. |
| māgno opere, *vehementer*. | cōgo, *condūco, 2*. |
| interest, *pertinet*. | cōgnōsco, *reperio, 4*. |
| distineo, *dīvido*. | mātūro, *propero*. |
| cōnflīgo : *pūgno, dīmico*. | commeātus, *cibus*. |

### How the Belgœ lay siege to a town.

6. Ab hīs castris oppidum Rēmōrum nōmine Bibrax
aberat mīlia passuum octo. Id ex itinere māgno impetu
Belgae oppūgnāre coepērunt. Aegre eo die sustentātum
est. Gallōrum eadem atque Belgārum oppūgnātio est
5 haec. Circumiecta multitūdine hominum tōtis moenibus
undique in mūrum lapides iaciunt. Ubi mūrus dēfēnsōribus nūdātus est, testūdine facta portas succēdunt mūrum-
que subruunt. Quod tum facile fīēbat. Nam cum tanta

multitūdo lapides āc tēla cōnicerent, in mūro cōnsistendi potestas erat nūlli. Postrēmo fīnem oppūgnandi nox 10 fēcit. Tum Iccius Rēmus, qui oppido praefuerat, nūntium ad Caesarem mittit: nisi subsidium sibi submittātur, sēse diūtius sustinēre nōn posse.

| | |
|---|---|
| tōtus, *omnis.* | subruo, *suffodio.* |
| undique, *ex omni parte.* | cōnsisto, *sto.* |
| ubi, *cum.* | praesum, *praefectus sum.* |
| nūdo, *privo.* | subsidium, *auxilium.* |
| succēdo: *accēdo, subeo.* | sustineo, *sustento.* |

*They abandon the siege and turn against Cæsar.*

**7.** Eo de media nocte Caesar Numidas et Crētas sagittārios et funditōres Baleāres subsidio oppidānis mittit; quōrum adventu hostibus spes potiundi oppidi discessit. Itaque paulisper apud oppidum morāti agrōsque Rēmōrum dēpopulāti ad castra Caesaris omnibus cōpiis con- 5 tendērunt et ab mīlibus passuum minus duōbus castra posuērunt; quae castra, ut fūmo atque īgnibus sīgnificābātur, amplius mīlibus passuum octo in lātitūdinem patēbant.

| | |
|---|---|
| subsidium, *auxilium,* 6. | moror, *cunctor.* |
| potior, *occupo.* | dēpopulor, *vāsto.* |
| discēdo, *abeo.* | contendo, *mātūro,* 5. |
| paulisper, *nōn diu.* | pateo, *pertineo.* |

*Cæsar awaits the attack of the enemy.*

**8.** Caesar prīmo propter multitūdinem hostium et propter eximiam opīniōnem virtūtis proelio supersedēre statuit: cotīdie tamen quid hostis virtūte posset et quid nostri audērent perīclitābātur. Locus erat pro castris ad aciem īnstruendam nātūra opportūnus atque idōneus. Is 5 autem collis, ubi castra posita erant, paululum ex plānitie

ēditus tantum adversus in lātitūdinem patēbat quantum
loci acies īnstrūcta occupāre poterat.  Atque ex utrāque
parte lateris dēiectus habēbat, et in frōntem lēniter fastī-
10 gātus paulātim ad plānitiem redībat.  Ab utrōque latere
ēius collis trānsversam fossam obdūxit circite͟r passuum
quadringeutōrum et ad extrēmas fossas castella cōnstituit
ibique tormenta conlocāvit, ne hostes ab lateribus pūg-
nantes suos circumvenīre possent.  Hōc facto duābus
15 legiōnibus quās proxime cōnscrīpserat in castris relīctis,
reliquas sex legiōnes pro castris in acie cōnstituit.  Hostes
item suas cōpias ex castris ēductas īnstrūxerant.

eximius : *excellens, ēgregius.*   idōneus : *aptus, commodus.*
opinio, *fāma.*   dēiectus, *declīvitas.*
supersedeo, *abstineo.*   fastīgātus, *adclīvis.*
periclitor : *tento, experior.*   conloco, *pōno.*

*Finally the enemy make a dash to cross the Axona.*

**9.**  Palus erat hōn māgna inter nostrum atque hostium
exercitum.  Hanc si nostri trānsīrent hostes exspectābant.  Interim proelio equestri inter duas acies contendēbātur.  Ubi neutri trānseundae ēius palūdis initium
5 faciunt, secundiōre equitum proelio nostris Caesar suos
in castra redūxit.  Hostes prōtinus ex eo loco ad flūmen
Axonam contendērunt, quod esse post nostra castra
dēmōnstrātum est.  Partem suārum cōpiārum trādūcere
cōnāti sunt, ut castellum cui praeerat Q. Titurius lēgātus
10 expūgnārent pontemque interscinderent; si minus potuissent, ut agros Rēmōrum populārentur commeātūque
nostros prohibērent.

initium, *prīncipium.*   contendo, *mātūro, 7.*
secundus, *prōsperus.*   praesum, *praefectus sum, 6.*
prōtinus : *statim, extemplo,*   interscindo, *abrumpo.*
    *repente, subito.*   commeātus, *cibus, 5.*

*A battle follows, the Belgæ are defeated and disperse.*

**10.** Caesar omnem equitātum et levis armātūrae Numidas, funditōres sagittāriōsque pontem trādūcit atque ad eos contendit. Ācriter in eo loco pūgnātum est. Hostes impedītos nostri in flūmine adgressi māgnum eōrum numerum occīdērunt. Prīmos qui trānsierant equitātu 5 circumventos interfēcērunt. Hostes, ubi de expūgnando oppido spem se fefellisse intellēxērunt neque nostros in locum inīquiōrem prōgredi viderunt atque ipsos res frūmentāria dēficere coepit, concilium convocāvērunt. Cōnstituērunt optimum esse domum suam quemque reverti. 10 Cōnstituērunt etiam ut quōrum in fīnes prīmum Rōmāni exercitum intrōdūxissent ad eos dēfendendos undique convenīrent. Quod eo cōnsilio fēcērunt, ut potius in suis quam in aliēnis fīnibus dēcertārent. Ad eam sententiam haec ratio eos dēdūxit, quod Divitiacum atque Aeduos 15 fīnibus Bellovacōrum adpropīnquāre cōgnōverant. Hīs persuādēri ut diūtius morārentur nōn poterat.

| | |
|---|---|
| armātūra, *arma.* | cōnstituo, *statuo.* |
| ācriter, *vehementer.* | revertor, *redeo.* |
| adgredior, *adorior.* | dēcerto : *pūgno, dīmico.* |
| occīdo, *concīdo.* | sententia, *cōnsilium.* |
| prōgredior : *prōcēdo, prōdeo.* | moror, *cunctor, 7.* |

*They are pursued with awful slaughter.*

**11.** Ea re cōnstitūta, secunda vigilia māgno cum strepitu āc tumultu castris ēgressi, nūllo certo ōrdine neque imperio, fēcērunt ut cōnsimilis fugae profectio vidērētur. Hāc re statim Caesar per speculātōres cōgnita īnsidiās veritus exercitum equitātumque castris continuit. Prīma 5 lūce omnem equitātum qui novissimum āgmen morārētur

praemīsit. T. Labiēnum lēgātum cum legiōnibus tribus subsequi iūssit. Hi novissimos adorti et multa mīlia passuum prōsecūti māgnam multitūdinem eōrum fugięn-
10 tium concīdērunt. Ii ad quos ventum erat cōnsistēbant fortiterque impetum nostrōrum sustinēbant; sed priōres, quod abesse a perīculo vidēbantur, exaudīto clāmōre perturbātis ōrdinibus omnes in fuga sibi praesidium pōnē-bant. Ita sine ūllo perīculo māgnam eōrum multitūdinem
15 nostri interfēcērunt sub occāsumque sōlis dēstitērunt sēque in castra, ut erat imperātum, recēpērunt.

| | |
|---|---|
| cōnstituo, *statuo*, 10. | subsequor : *prōsequor,* ī*nsequor.* |
| strepitus : *clāmor, fremitus.* | adorior, *adgredior,* 10. |
| cōnsimilis, *persimilis.* | concīdo, *occīdo,* 10. |
| vereor, *timeo,* 1. | cōnsisto, *sto,* 6. |
| moror, *cunctor,* 7. | sustineo, *sustento,* 6. |

*A forced march and attack on Noviodunum. The town surrenders.*

**12.** Postrīdie ēius diēi Caesar' in fīnes Suessiōnum exercitum dūxit et māgno itinere cōnfecto ad oppĭdum Noviodūnum contendiţ Id ex itinere oppūgnāre cōnātus, quod vacuum ab dēfēnsōribus esse audiēbat, expūgnāre
5 nōn potuit. Interim omnis ex fuga Suessiōnum multi-tūdo in oppidum proxima nocte convēnit. Celeriter vīneis ad oppidum āctis, aggere iacto turribusque cōnstitūtis, māgnitūdine operum et celeritāte Rōmānōrum permōti sunt Suessiōnes. Itaque lēgātos ad Caesarem de dēdi-
10 tiōne mittunt et petentibus Rēmis ut cōnservārentur im-petrant.

| | |
|---|---|
| cōnficio, *perficio.* | ago : *pello, dūco, traho.* |
| contendo, *propero.* | permoveo, *commoveo.* |
| vacuus : *carens, nūdus.* | dēditio, *trāditio.* |
| interim, *interea.* | impetro, *cōnsequor.* |

*The Bellovaci also submit at Cæsar's approach.*

**13.** Caesar obsidibus acceptis armīsque omnibus ex oppido trāditis in dēditiōnem Suessiōnes accēpit exercitumque in Bellovacos dūxit. Qui cum se suaque omnia in oppidum Bratuspantium contulissent, atque ab eo oppido Caesar cum exercitu circiter mīlia passuum quīn- 5 que abesset, omnes māiōres nātu ex oppido ēgressi manus ad Caesarem tendere et vōce sīgnificāre coepērunt sēse in ēius fidem āc potestātem venīre./ Item, cum ad oppidum accessisset, pueri mulierēsque ex mūro passis manibus suo mōre pācem ab Rōmānis petiērunt. 10

trādo: *do, dēdo.*  
me cōnfero: *me recipio, eo.*  
ēgredior, *exeo.*  
coepi, *incēpi.*

pueri, *līberi.*  
pando, *tendo.*  
mōs, *cōnsuētūdo.*  
peto, *ōro.*

*Divitiacus pleads earnestly for the Bellovaci.*

**14.** Pro hīs Divitiacus facit verba: "Bellovaci omni tempore in fide atque amīcitia cīvitātis Aeduae fuērunt: impulsi a suis prīncipibus, qui dīcēbant Aeduos omnes indīgnitātes contumēliāsque perferre, ab Aeduis dēfēcērunt et populo Rōmāno bellum intulērunt. Ii qui ēius 5 cōnsili prīncipes fuērunt in Britanniam profūgērunt. Petunt nōn sōlum Bellovaci sed etiam pro hīs Aedui ut tua clēmentia āc mānsuētūdine in eos ūtāris. Quod si fēceris, Aeduōrum auctōritātem apud omnes Belgas amplificābis, quōrum auxiliis atque opibus, si qua bella 10 incidunt, sustentāre cōnsuērunt."

impello: *incito, indūco.*  
contumēlia, *iniūria.*  
dēficio: *dēsero.*  
mānsuētūdo, *lēnitas.*

auctōritas, *grātia.*  
amplifico, *augeo.*  
sustento, *sustineo, 6.*  
cōnsuēsco, *soleo.*

*The temperance, courage, and patriotism of the Nervii.*

**15.** Caesar honōris Divitiaci atque Aeduōrum causa sēse eos in fidem receptūrum et cōnservātūrum dīxit; quod erat cīvitas māgna inter Belgas auctōritāte, sexcentos obsides poposcit. Hīs trāditis omnibusque armis 5 ex oppido conlātis, ab eo loco in fīnes Ambiānōrum pervēnit. Eōrum fīnes Nervii attingēbant; quōrum de nātūra mōribusque Caesar cum quaereret, sīc reperiēbat: Nūllus aditus erat ad eos mercātōribus; nihil patiebantur vīni reliquārumque rērum īnferri, quod iis rēbus 10 relanguēscere animos et remitti virtūtem exīstimābant: erant homines feri māgnaeque virtūtis; increpitābant atque incūsābant reliquos Belgas, qui se populo Rōmāno dēdidissent.

auctōritas, *grātia*, 14.
posco, *impero*.
cōnfero, *cōgo*, 2.
attingo, *contingo*.
aditus, *accessus*.

patior, *sino*.
relanguēsco, *effēminor*.
remitto, *minuo*.
incūso, *accūso*.
dēdo, *permitto*.

*Encamped on the Sabis the Nervii await the coming of Cæsar.*

**16.** Cum per eōrum fīnes trīduum iter fēcisset, inveniēbat ex captīvis Sabim flūmen ab castris suis nōn amplius mīlia passuum x abesse. Trāns id flūmen omnes Nervii cōnsēderant adventumque ibi Rōmānōrum exspec-5 tābant. Exspectābantur etiam ab hīs Aduātucōrum cōpiae atque erant in itinere. Mulieres quīque per aetātem ad pūgnam inūtiles vidērentur in eum locum coniēcerant, quo propter palūdes exercitui aditus nōn esset.

cōnsīdo, *me colloco*, 4.   cōnicio, *dēpōno*.   aditus, 15.

*They plan to attack Caesar's advance guard.*

**17.** Hīs rēbus cōgnitīs explōrātōrēs centuriōnēsque praemittit quī locum idōneum castrīs dēligant. Cum ex dēditīciīs Belgīs reliquīsque Gallīs complūrēs Caesarem secūtī ūna iter facerent, quīdam ex hīs nocte ad Nerviōs pervēnērunt. Hīs dēmōnstrārunt inter singulās legiōnēs 5 impedīmentōrum māgnum numerum intercēdere, neque esse quicquam negōtī, cum prīma legiō in castra vēnisset, hanc sub sarcinīs adorīrī; quā pulsā futūrum ut reliquae legiōnēs contra cōnsistere nōn audērent. Nerviī autem antīquitus, quō facilius fīnitimōrum equitātum impedī- 10 rent, teneris arboribus incīsīs atque īnflexīs, crēbrīsque in lātitūdinem rāmis ēnātīs, et rubīs sentibusque inter- iectīs, effēcerant ut īnstar mūrī hae saepēs mūnīmenta praebērent, quō nōn modo nōn intrārī sed ne perspicī quidem posset. Hīs rēbus cum iter āgminis nostri im- 15 pedīrētur, nōn omittendum sibi cōnsilium Nerviī exīsti- māvērunt.

| | |
|---|---|
| **idōneus**: *aptus, commodus*, 8. | **cōnsisto**, *sto*, 8. |
| **dēligo**, *ēligo*. | **incido**, *accīdo*. |
| **intercēdo**, *intervenio*. | **īnstar**: *forma, similitūdo*. |
| **sarcinae**: *impedīmenta, onera*. | **omitto**, *neglego*. |
| **adorior**, *adgredior*, 11. | **exīstimo**, *puto*. |

*The Roman camping-ground and the position of the enemy.*

**18.** Locī nātūra erat haec, quem locum nostrī castrīs dēlēgerant. Collis ab summō aequāliter dēclīvis ad flūmen Sabim, quod supra nōmināvimus, vergēbat. Ab eō flū- mine parī adclīvitāte collis nāscēbātur, ab superiōre parte silvestris ut nōn facile intrōrsus perspicī posset. Intra 5 eas silvas hostēs in occultō sēse continēbant; in apertō

loco secundum flūmen paucae statiōnes equitum vidēbantur. Flūminis erat altitūdo pedum circiter trium.

| | |
|---|---|
| **summum,** *culmen.* | **intrōrsus,** *intra.* |
| **dēclīvis,** *prōclīvis.* | **in occulto,** *abditus.* |
| **vergo,** *pertineo.* | **statio,** *custōdia.* |
| **nāscor,** *orior,* 4. | **circiter,** *ad.* |

*The plan of attack is skilfully carried out by the Nervii.*

**19.** Caesar equitātu praemīsso subsequēbātur omnibus cōpiis. Sed quod ad hostes adpropinquābat, cōnsuētūdine sua sex legiōnes expedītas dūcēbat; post eas
tōtīus exercitus impedīmenta conlocārat; inde duae legi-
5 ōnes, quae proxime cōnscrīptae erant, tōtum āgmen clau-
dēbant praesidiōque impedīmentis erant. Equites nostri,
cum funditōribus sagittāriīsque flūmen trānsgressi, cum
hostium equitātu proelium commīsērunt. Illi se identidem in silvas ad suos recipiēbant āc rūrsus ex silva in
10 nostros impetum faciēbant. Interim legiōnes sex, quae
prīmae vēnerant, opere dīmēnso castra mūnīre coepērunt.
Ubi prīma impedīmenta nostri exercitus ab iis qui in
silvis abditi latēbant vīsa sunt, subito omnibus cōpiis
prōvolāvērunt impetumque in nostros equites fēcērunt.
15 Hīs facile pulsis āc prōturbātis, incrēdibili celeritāte ad
flūmen dēcucurrērunt, ut paene ūno tempore ad silvas et
in flūmine et iam in manibus nostris hostes vidērentur.
Eādem autem celeritāte adverso colle ad nostra castra
atque eos qui in opere occupāti erant contendērunt.

| | |
|---|---|
| **subsequor,** *prōsequor,* 11. | **dīmētior,** *mētior.* |
| **conloco,** *pōno,* 8. | **lateo,** *me cēlo.* |
| **trānsgredior,** *trānseo.* | **prōvolo,** *prōruo.* |
| **identidem,** *iterum atque iterum.* | **prōturbo,** *fugo.* |
| **rūrsus,** *iterum.* | **paene,** *fere.* |
| **interim,** *interea,* 12. | **contendo,** *propero,* 7. |

*But the soldiers and lieutenants know what to do.*

**20.** Caesari omnia ūno tempore erant agenda: vēxillum prōpōnendum, sīgnum tuba dandum, ab opere revocandi mīlites, acies īnstruenda, mīlites cohortandi, sīgnum dandum. Quārum rērum māgnam partem temporis brevitas et successus hostium impediēbat. Sed erat subsidio 5 scientia atque ūsus mīlitum, quod superiōribus proeliis exercitāti, nōn minus commode. ipsi sibi praescrībere quam ab aliis docēri poterant. Praeterea ab opere singulīsque legiōnibus singulos lēgātos Caesar discēdere vetuerat. Hi propter propīnquitātem et celeritātem 10 hostium nihil iam Caesaris imperium exspectābant, sed per se quae vidēbantur administrābant.

| | |
|---|---|
| **prōpōno,** *ostendo.* | **commodē** : *apte, bene.* |
| **successus,** *accessus,* 15. | **praescrībo,** *praecipio.* |
| **subsidium,** *auxilium,* 6. | **veto,** *prohibeo.* |
| **ūsus,** *experientia.* | **propīnquitas,** *vīcīnitas.* |
| **exercitātus,** *perītus.* | **administro** : *prōvideo, ago.* |

*Fighting begins before the soldiers can arm themselves.*

**21.** Caesar necessāriis rēbus imperātis ad cohortandos mīlites dēcucurrit et ad legiōnem decimam ' dēvēnit. Mīlites nōn longiōre ōrātiōne cohortātus quam uti suae prīstinae virtūtis memoriam retinērent neu perturbārentur animo hostiumque impetum fortiter sustinērent, 5 quod nōn lónge hostes aberant, proeli committendi sīgnum dedit Atque in alteram pártem item cohortandi causa prófectus pūguantibus occurrit Temporis tanta fuit exiguitas hostiumque tam parātus ad dīmicandum animus, ut nōn modo ad īnsīgnia adcommodanda, sed 10 etiam ad galeas induendas scūtīsque tegimenta dētrūdenda tempus dēfuerit, Quam in partem quisque ab opere cāsu dēvēnit quaeque prīma sīgna cōnspēxit, ad haec cōnstitit, ne in quaerendis suis pūgnandi tempus dīmitteret.

| | |
|---|---|
| **dēvenio,** *pervenio.* | **adcommodo,** *apto.* |
| **prīstinus**: *vetus, antīquus.* | **induo,** *indūco.* |
| **perturbo,** *commoveo,* 12. | **dētrūdo,** *dētraho.* |
| **sustineo,** *sustento,* 6. | **cāsu,** *fŏrte.* |
| **occurro,** *incĭdo.* | **cōnspicio,** *cōnspicor.* |
| **exiguitas,** *brevitas.* | **dīmitto,** *āmitto.* |

*All is confusion in the battle; the commander can do little.*

**22.** Īnstrūcto exercitu magis ut loci nātūra dēiectusque collis et necessitas temporis quam ut rei mīlitāris ratio atque ōrdo postulābat, fīebat ut aliae legiōnes alia in parte hostibus resisterent; saepibus autem dēnsissimis,

5 ut ante dēmōnstrāvimus, interiectis prōspectus impediēbātur, ut neque certa subsidia conlocāri, neque ab ūnc omnia imperia administrāri possent. Itaque in tanta rērum inīquitāte, fōrtūnae quoque ēventus varii sequēbantur.

| | |
|---|---|
| **dēiectus,** *dēclīvitas,* 8. | **administro,** *ago,* 20. |
| **ratio,** *scientia.* | **inīquitas,** *varietas.* |
| **intericio,** *interpōno.* | . **ēventus,** *cāsus.* |

*The battle seems to be going against Cæsar.*

**23.** Legiōnis nōnae et decimae mīlites, ut in sinistra parte acie cōnstiterant, Atrebates cursu āc lassitūdine exanimātos vulneribusque cōnfectos celeriter ex loco superiōre in flūmen compulērunt. Tum eos trānsīre

5 cōnantes īnsecūti, gladiis māgnam partem eōrum interfēcērunt. Ipsi trānsīre flūmen nōn dubitāvērunt et in locum inīquum prōgressi, hostes redintegrātō proelio in fugam cōniēcērunt. Item alia in parte dīversae duae legiōnes, ūndecima et octāva, ex loco superiōre in ipsis

flūminis rīpis proeliābantur. At tōtis fere a frōnte et ab sinistra parte nūdātis castris, omnes Nervii cōnfertissimo āgmine, duce Boduōgnāto, qui summam imperi tenēbat, ad eum locum contendērunt; quōrum pars aperto latere legiōnes circumvenīre, pars summum castrōrum locum petere coepit.

| | |
|---|---|
| lassitūdo, *dēfatīgātio.* | cōnfertus, *dēnsus.* |
| cōnfectus, *dēfessus.* | summa, *cūra,* 4. |
| compello, *ago.* | contendo, *propero,* 12. |
| redintegro, *renovo.* | peto, *accurro.* |

*It is beginning to look very dark for the Romans.*

24. Eōdem tempore equites nostri levisque armātūrae pedites, qui cum iis ūna fuerant, cum se in castra reciperent, hostibus occurrēbant ăc rūrsus aliam in partem fugam petēbant; et cālōnes, praedandi causa ēgressi, cum respēxissent et hostes in nostris castris versāri vīdissent, praecipites fugae sēse mandābant, Simul eōrum qui cum impedīmentis veniēbant clāmor fremitusque oriēbātur, aliīque aliam in partem perterriti ferēbantur. Quibus omnibus rēbus permōti sunt equites Trēveri, qui auxili causa ab cīvitāte ad Caesarem mīssi vēnerant. Ergo cum multitūdine hostium castra complēri, legiones premi et paene circumventas tenēri, cālōnes, equites, funditōres in omnes partes fugere vīdissent, dēspērātis nostris rēbus, domum contendērunt atque Rōmānos pulsos superātōsque cīvitāti renūntiāvērunt.

| | |
|---|---|
| armātūra, *arma,* 10. | fremitus, *strepitus,* 11. |
| me recipio, *me cōnfero,* 13. | orior, *nāscor,* 4. |
| occurro, *incĭdo,* 21. | premo, *urgeo.* |
| ēgredior, *exeo,* 13. | paene, *fere,* 19. |
| versor, *sum occupātus,* 1. | pello : *fugo, prōturbo,* 19. |
| mando, *commendo.* | supero, *vinco.* |

*Will Cæsar's coolness and courage save his army?*

**25.** Caesar ab decimae legiōnis cohortātiōne ad dextrum cornu profectus suos urgēri et duodecimae legiōnis cōnfertos mīlites sibi ipsos ad pūgnam esse impedīmento vīdit. Quartae cohortis omnes centuriōnes occīsi sunt
5 et, sĩgnifero interfecto, sīgnum est āmīssum. Reliquārum cohortium omnes fere centuriōnes aut vulnerāti aut occīsi sunt, in hīs prīmipīlus P. Sextius Baculus, fortissimus vir, multis gravibusque vulneribus cōnfectus ut iam se sustinēre nōn posset. Hīs rēbus reliquos esse tardiōres
10 vīdit Caesar et nōnnūllos dēserto proelio excēdere āc tēla vītāre; hostes autem neque a fronte ex īnferiōre loco subeuntes intermittere et ab utrōque latere īnstāre, et rem esse in angusto, neque ūllum esse subsidium quod submitti posset. Tum vēro scūto ūni mīliti dētracto,
15 quod ipse eo sine scūto vēnerat, in prīmam aciem prōcessit, centuriōnibusque nōminātim appellātis, reliquos cohortātus mīlites sīgna īnferre et manipulos laxāre iũssit, quo facilius gladiis ūti possent. Cūius adventu spe inlāta mīlitibus āc redintegrāto animo paulum hostium impetus
20 tardātus est.

| | |
|---|---|
| **urgeo,** *premo,* 24. | **subeo,** *succēdo.* |
| **cōnfertus,** *dēnsus,* 23. | **intermitto :** *dēsino, dēsisto.* |
| **sīgnifer,** *aquilifer.* | **īnsto :** *urgeo, premo,* 24. |
| **āmitto,** *dīmitto,* 21. | **dētraho,** *rapio.* |
| **fere,** *paene,* 19. | **laxo,** *aperio.* |
| **cōnfectus,** *dēfessus,* 23. | **īnfero** (2): *do, adfero.* |
| **excēdo,** *exeo.* | **redintegro,** *renovo,* 23. |

*A shifting scene.* **Pull Romans, pull Nervii!**

**26.** Caesar cum septimam legiōnem, quae iũxta cōnstiterat, item urgēri ab hoste vīdisset, tribūnos mīlitum monuit ut paulātim sēse legiōnes coniungerent. Quo

facto, cum alius alii subsidium ferret, audācius resistere
āc fortius pūgnāre coepērunt. Interim mīlites legiōnum 5
duārum, quae in novissimo āgmine praesidio impedīmentis fuerant, proelio nūntiāto cursu incitāto in summo colle
ab hostibus cōnspiciēbantur et T. Labiēnus castris hostium potītus decimam legiōnem subsidio nostris mīsit.
Qui cum quo in loco res esset, quantōque in perīculo cas- 10
tra et legiōnes et imperātor versārētur, cōgnōvissent,
nihil ad celeritātem sibi reliqui fēcērunt

| | | |
|---|---|---|
| **iūxta**, *prope.* | **paulātim**, *gradātim.* | **potior**, *occupo*, 7. |
| **cōnsisto**, 6. | **interim**, *interea*, 12. | **versor**, *sum*, 1. |
| **urgeo**, 25. | **cōnspicio**, *video.* | **cōgnōsco**, *reperio*, 4. |

*In the fierce wrestle the brave Nervii go under.*

27. Hōrum adventu tanta rērum commūtātio est facta
ut nostri, etiam qui vulneribus cōnfecti prōcubuissent,
proelium redintegrārent; equites vēro, ut turpitūdinem
fugae virtūte dēlērent, omnibus in locis pūgnae se legiō-
nāriis mīlitibus praeferrent. At hostes etiam in extrēma 5
spe salūtis māximam virtutem praestitērunt; nam cum
prīmi eōrum cecidissent, proximi iacentibus comitibus
īnsistēbant atque ex eōrum corporibus pūgnābant; hīs
dēiectis et coacervātis cadāveribus, cēteri ut ex tumulo
tēla in nostros cōniciēbant et pīla intercepta remittēbant, 10
ut iūdicāri dēbēret nōn nēquīquam tantae virtūtis homines ausos esse trānsīre lātissimum flūmen, ascendere altissimas rīpas, subīre inīquissimum locum: quae facilia ex
difficillimis animi māgnitūdo redēgerat.

| | |
|---|---|
| **prōcumbo**, *prōcido.* | **iaceo**, *prōcumbo.* |
| **turpitūdo** : *ignōminia*, *īnfāmia.* | **coacervo** : *congero*, *cōgo.* |
| **dēleo**, *exstinguo.* | **cadāver**, *corpus.* |
| **extrēmus**, *ultimus.* | **nēquīquam**, *frūstra.* |
| **praesto** : *praebeo*, *ostento.* | **redigo**, *facio.* |

*Why slay the poor remnant ?  Let them live.*

**28.** Hōc proelio facto et prope ad interneciōnem gente āc nōmine Nerviōrum redācto, māiōres nātu, quōs ūna cum pueris mulieribusque in palūdes cōniectos dīxerāmus, cōnsēnsu omnium qui supererant lēgātos ad Caesarem 5 mīsērunt sēque ei dēdidērunt. Postea in commemoranda cīvitātis calamitāte, ex sexcentis ad tres senātōres, ex hominum mīlibus LX vix ad quīngentos qui arma ferre possent, sēse redāctos esse dīxērunt, Quōs Caesar ut in miseros āc supplices ūsus misericordia vidērētur, dīli- 10 gentissime cōnservāvit suīsque fīnibus atque oppidis ūti iūssit et fīnitimis imperāvit ut ab iniūria et maleficio se suōsque prohibērent.

| | |
|---|---|
| **prope,** *paene,* 19. | **cōnicio,** *dēpōno,* 16. |
| **internecio,** *interitus.* | **dēdo,** *permitto,* 15. |
| **redigo,** *redūco.* | **commemoro,** *nārro.* |
| **pueri,** *līberi,* 13. | **finitimus,** *vicīnus,* 2. |

*The Aduatuci prepare to make a desperate resistance.*

**29.** Aduātuci, qui cum omnibus cōpiis auxilio Nerviis veniēbant, hāc pūgna nūntiāta ex itinere domum revertē- runt; cūnctis oppidis castellīsque dēsertis sua omnia in ūnum oppidum ēgregie nātūra mūnītum contulērunt. 5 Quod ex omnibus in circuitu partibus altissimas rūpes dēspectūsque habēbat, sed ūna ex parte lēniter adclīvis aditus relinquēbātur; quem locum duplici altissimo mūro mūnierant; tum māgni ponderis saxa et praeacūtas trabes in mūro conlocābant, Ipsi erant ex Cimbris Teutonīsque 10 prōgnāti, qui, cum iter in prōvinciam nostram atque Ītaliam facerent, custōdiam ex suis āc praesidium sex mīlia hominum relīquērunt. Hi post eōrum obitum

multos annos a fīnitimis exagitāti, cōnsēnsu eōrum omnium hunc sibi domicilio locum dēlēgērunt.

| | |
|---|---|
| **revertor,** *redeo*, 10. | **aditus,** *accessus*, 15. |
| **cūnctus,** *omnis.* | **conloco,** *pōno*, 8. |
| **ēgregie:** *optime, eximie*, 8. | **prōgnātus,** *ortus*, 4. |
| **dēspectus,** *prōspectus.* | **obitus,** *interitus*, 28. |
| **lēniter,** *paulātim.* | **dēligo,** *ēligo*, 17. |

*From their walls they taunt the Romans.*

**30.** Ac prīmo adventu exercitus nostri crēbras ex
oppido excursiōnes faciēbant parvulīsque proeliis cum
nostris contendēbant; postea vāllo pedum xii in circuitu
xv mīlium crēbrīsque castellis circummūnīti oppido sēse
continēbant. Ubi vīneis āctis aggere exstrūcto turrim  5
procul cōnstitui vīdērunt, prīmum inrīdēre ex mūro atque
increpitāre vōcibus coepērunt, quod tanta māchinātio ab
tanto spatio īnstruerētur: quibusnam manibus aut quibus vīribus praesertim homines tantulae statūrae turrim
tanti oneris in mūro sēse conlocāre cōnfīderent?    10

| | |
|---|---|
| **adventus,** *accessus*, 15. | **inrīdeo,** *dērīdeo.* |
| **crēber,** *frequens*, 1. | **increpito,** *maledīco.* |
| **excursio,** *ēruptio.* | **tantulus,** *parvulus.* |
| **cōnstituo,** *pōno.* | **onus,** *pondus.* |

*But soon they lose confidence and offer to surrender.*

**31.** Ubi vēro turrim movēri et adpropīnquāre moenibus vīdērunt, nova atque inūsitāta specie commōti lēgātos
ad Caesarem de pāce mīsērunt, qui ad hunc modum locūti
sunt: Aduātuci nōn exīstimant Rōmānos sine ope dīvīna
bellum gerere, qui tantae altitūdinis māchinātiōnes tanta  5
celeritāte prōmovēre possint; itaque se suaque omnia
eōrum potestāti permittunt. Ūnum petunt: si fōrte

Caesar pro sua clēmentia ăc mānsuētūdine statuerit Aduātucos esse cōnservandos, ne eos armis dēspoliet. ₁₀ Omnes fere fīnitimi sunt inimīci ăc eōrum virtūti invident, a quibus se dēfendere trāditis armis nōn poterunt. Sibi praestet, si in eum cāsum dēdūcantur, quamvis fōrtūnam a populo Rōmāno pati, quam ab inimīcis per cruciātum interfici.

novus, *mīrus.*

inūsitātus : *īnsolitus, novus.*

species, *facies.*

modus, *ratio.*

ops, *auxilium.*

permitto, *dēdo,* 15.

peto, *ōro,* 13.

mānsuētūdo, *lēnitas,* 14.

statuo, *cōnstituo,* 10.

fere, *paene,* 25.

cāsus, *fātum,* 22.

dēdūco, *redigo,* 28.

*They must disarm, but are promised protection.*

**32.** Ad haec Caesar respondit: "Magis cōnsuētūdine mea quam merito vestro cīvitātem cōnservābo, si prius quam mūrum aries attigerit, vos dēdideritis: sed dēditiōnis nūlla est condicio nisi armis trāditis. Id quod in ₅ Nerviis fēci faciam fīnitimīsque imperābo ne quam iniūriam dēditīciis populi Rōmāni īnferant." Re nūntiāta ad suos, quae imperārentur facere dīxērunt. Armōrum tanta multitūdo de mūro in fossam quae erat ante oppidum iacta est, ut propé summam mūri aggerisque alti- ₁₀ tūdinem acervi eōrum adaequārent, et tamen circiter pars tertia, ut postea perspectum est, cēlāta atque in oppido retenta est. Deinde portis patefactis eo die pāce sunt ūsi oppidāni.

prius quam, *ante quam.*

dēditio, *trāditio,* 12.

fīnitimus, *vīcīnus,* 2.

īnfero : *fero, facio.*

prope, *paene,* 28.

circiter, *ad,* 19.

perspicio, *intellego.*

patefacio, *aperio.*

*A brave dash for freedom, but a terrible fate.*

**33.** Sub vesperum Caesar portas claudi mīlitēsque ex oppido exīre iūssit. Oppidānī cōnsilio ante inito, ut intellēctum est, quod dēditiōne facta nostros praesidia dēductūros aut dēnique indīligentius servātūros crēdiderant, tertia vigilia, qua minime arduus ad nostras mūnī- 5 tiōnes ascēnsus vidēbātur, omnibus cōpiis repentīno ex oppido ēruptiōnem fēcērunt. Celeriter, ut ante Caesar imperārat, īgnibus sīgnificātiōne facta ex proximis castellis eo concursum est. Ibi pūgnātum est ācriter ab hostibus in extrēma spe salūtis inīquo loco contra eos 10 qui ex vāllo turribusque tēla iacerent, cum in ūna virtūte omnis spes salūtis cōnsisteret. Occīsis ad hominum mīlibus quattuor reliqui in oppidum reiecti sunt. Postrīdie ēius diēi refrāctis portis, cum iam dēfenderet nēmo, atque intrōmīssis mīlitibus nostris sectiōnem ēius oppidi 15 ūniversam Caesar vendidit. Ab iis qui ēmerant capitum numerus ad eum relātus est mīlium quīnquāginta trium.

intellego, *perspicio;* 82.     ēruptio, *excursio,* 30.
dēnique, *saltem.*     sīgnificātio, *signum.*
indīligenter, *neglegenter.*     inīquus, *incommodus.*
arduus, *difficilis.*     ūniversus, *tōtus.*
repentīnus, *subitus.*     refero, *renūntio.*

*All the maritime nations submit to the Romans.*

**34.** Eōdem tempore a P. Crasso, quem cum legiōne ūna mīserat ad Venetos, Unellos, Osismos, Curiosolitas, Esuvios, Aulercos, Rēdones, quae sunt maritimae cīvitātes Ōceanumque attingunt, certior factus est omnes eas cīvitātes in diciōnem potestātemque populi Rōmāni esse 5 redāctas.

attingo, *tango.*     dicio, *imperium.*     redigo, *pāco.*

*Gaul lies crushed and bleeding. Rome rejoices and thanks
the gods.*

**35.** Hīs rēbus gestis omni Gallia pācāta, tanta hūius
belli ad barbaros opīnio perlāta est uti ab iis nātiōnibus
quae trāns Rhēnum incolerent mitterentur lēgāti ad
Caesarem, qui se obsides datūras, imperāta factūras polli-
5 cērentur. Quās lēgātiōnes Caesar, quod in Ītaliam Illyri-
cumque properābat, inita proxima aestāte ad se reverti
iūssit. Ipse in Carnūtes, Andes Turonēsque, quae cīvitātes propīnquae hīs locis erant ubi bellum gesserat,
legiōnibus in hībernācula dēductis, in Ītaliam profectus
10 est. Ob eāsque res ex litteris Caesaris dies quīndecim
supplicātio dēcrēta est, quod ante id tempus accidit nūlli.

| | |
|---|---|
| pāco, *redigo*, 34. | ineo, *incipio.* |
| opīnio, *fāma*, 8. | propīnquus : *vicīnus, finitimus,* 2. |
| propero, *mātūro*, 5. | accido, *contingo.* |

# C. IULI CAESARIS
# DE BELLO GALLICO

*LIBER SECUNDUS.*

B.C. 57; A.U.C. 697.

### THE BELGIAN LEAGUE DEFEATED.

**1.** Cum esset Caesar in citeriore Gallia in hibernis, ita
uti supra demonstravimus, crebri ad eum rumores adfere-
bantur, litterisque item Labieni certior fiebat omnes Belgas, quam tertiam esse Galliae partem dixeramus, contra
populum Romanum coniurare obsidesque inter se dare. 5
Coniurandi has esse causas: primum quod vererentur ne
omni pacata Gallia ad eos exercitus noster adduceretur;
deinde quod ab nonnullis Gallis sollicitarentur, — partim
qui, ut Germanos diutius in Gallia versari noluerant,
ita populi Romani exercitum hiemare atque invetera- 10
scere in Gallia moleste ferebant; partim qui mobilitate
et levitate animi novis imperiis studebant; ab nonnullis
etiam, quod in Gallia a potentioribus atque iis qui ad
conducendos homines facultates habebant, vulgo regna
occupabantur, qui minus facile eam rem imperio nostro 15
consequi poterant.

**2.** His nuntiis litterisque commotus Caesar duas legiones in citeriore Gallia novas conscripsit, et inita aestate
in interiorem Galliam qui deduceret Q. Pedium legatum
misit. Ipse, cum primum pabuli copia esse inciperet, 20

ad exercitum venit. Dat negotium Senonibus reliquisque
Gallis, qui finitimi Belgis erant, uti ea quae apud eos
gerantur cognoscant seque de his rebus certiorem faciant. Hi constanter omnes nuntiaverunt manus cogi, ex-
5 ercitum in unum locum conduci. Tum vero dubitandum
non existimavit quin ad eos proficisceretur. Re frumentaria comparata castra movet diebusque circiter quindecim ad fines Belgarum pervenit.

**3.** Eo cum de improviso celeriusque omni opinione
10 venisset, Remi, qui proximi Galliae ex Belgis sunt, ad
eum legatos Iccium et Andocumborium primos civitatis
miserunt qui dicerent: 'Se suaque omnia in fidem atque
in potestatem populi Romani permittere, neque se cum
Belgis reliquis consensisse neque contra populum Ro-
15 manum coniurasse, paratosque esse et obsides dare et
imperata facere et oppidis recipere et frumento ceteris-
que rebus iuvare; reliquos omnes Belgas in armis esse,
Germanosque qui cis Rhenum incolant sese cum his
coniunxisse, tantumque esse eorum omnium furorem ut
20 ne Suessiones quidem, fratres consanguineosque suos, qui
eodem iure et isdem legibus utantur, unum imperium
unumque magistratum cum ipsis habeant, deterrere po-
tuerint quin cum his consentirent.'

**4.** Cum ab his quaereret quae civitates quantaeque in
25 armis essent et quid in bello possent, sic reperiebat:
plerosque Belgas esse ortos ab Germanis Rhenumque
antiquitus traductos propter loci fertilitatem ibi consedisse Gallosque qui ea loca incolerent expulisse, solosque
esse qui patrum nostrorum memoria, omni Gallia vexata,
30 Teutonos Cimbrosque intra fines suos ingredi prohibu-
erint; qua ex re fieri uti earum rerum memoria magnam sibi auctoritatem magnosque spiritus in re militari

sumerent. De numero eorum omnia se habere explorata Remi dicebant, propterea quod propinquitatibus adfinitatibusque coniuncti, quantam quisque multitudinem in communi Belgarum concilio ad id bellum pollicitus sit cognoverint. Plurimum inter eos Bellovacos et virtute 5 et auctóritate et hominum numero valere : hos posse conficere armata milia centum, pollicitos ex eo numero electa sexaginta, totiusque belli imperium sibi postulare. Suessiones suos esse finitimos : latíssimos feracissimosque agros possidere. Apud eos fuisse regem nostra etiam 10 memoria Divitiacum, totius Galliae potentissimum, qui cum magnae partis harum regionum tum etiam Britanniae imperium obtinuerit : nunc esse regem Galbam ; ad hunc propter iustitiam prudentiamque suam totius belli summam omnium voluntate deferri : oppida habere nu- 15 mero xii, polliceri milia armata quinquaginta ; totidem Nervios, qui maxime feri inter ipsos habeantur, longissimeque absint ; quindecim milia Atrebates, Ambianos decem milia, Morinos xxv milia, Menapios vii milia ; Caletos x milia ; Velocasses et Veromanduos totidem ; 20 Aduatucos decem et novem milia ; Condrusos, Eburones, Caeroesos, Paemanos, qui uno nomine Germani appellantur, arbitrari ad xl milia.

**5.** Caesar Remos cohortatus liberaliterque oratione prosecutus omnem senatum ad se convenire principum- 25 que liberos obsides ad se adduci iussit. Quae omnia ab his diligenter ad diem facta sunt. Ipse Divitiacum Aeduum magno opere cohortatus docet quanto opere rei publicae communisque salutis intersit manus hostium distineri, ne cum tanta multitudine uno tempore confli- 30 gendum sit. Id fieri posse, si suas copias Aedui in fines Bellovacorum introduxerint et eorum agros populari coe-

perint. His mandatis eum ab se dimittit. Postquam
omnes Belgarum copias in unum locum coactas ad se
venire vidit neque iam longe abesse ab iis quos miserat
exploratoribus et ab Remis cognovit, flumen Axonam,
5 quod est in extremis Remorum finibus, exercitum traducere maturavit atque ibi castra posuit. Quae res et
latus unum castrorum ripis fluminis muniebat et post
eum quae essent tuta ab hostibus reddebat, et commeatus
ab Remis reliquisque civitatibus ut sine periculo ad eum
10 portari posset efficiebat. In eo flumine pons erat. Ibi
praesidium ponit et in altera parte fluminis Q. Titurium
Sabinum legatum cum sex cohortibus relinquit. Castra
in altitudinem pedum XII vallo fossaque duodeviginti
pedum munire iubet.

15 **6.** Ab his castris oppidum Remorum nomine Bibrax
aberat milia passuum octo. Id ex itinere magno impetu
Belgae oppugnare coeperunt. Aegre eo die sustentatum
est. Gallorum eadem atque Belgarum oppugnatio est
haec. Ubi circumiecta multitudine hominum totis moe-
20 nibus undique in murum lapides iaci coepti sunt, mu-
rusque defensoribus nudatus est, testudine facta portas
succedunt murumque subruunt. Quod tum facile fiebat.
Nam cum tanta multitudo lapides ac tela conicerent, in
muro consistendi potestas erat nulli. Cum finem oppug-
25 nandi nox fecisset, Iccius Remus, summa nobilitate et
gratia inter suos, qui tum oppido praefuerat, unus ex iis
qui legati de pace ad Caesarem venerant, nuntium ad
eum mittit: nisi subsidium sibi submittatur, sese diutius
sustinere non posse.

30 **7.** Eo de media nocte Caesar isdem ducibus usus qui
nuntii ab Iccio venerant, Numidas et Cretas sagittarios
et funditores Baleares subsidio oppidanis mittit; quorum

adventu et Remis cum spe defensionis studium propug-
nandi accessit, et hostibus eadem de causa spes potiundi
oppidi discessit. Itaque paulisper apud oppidum morati
agrosque Remorum depopulati, omnibus vicis aedificiis-
que quos adire potuerant incensis, ad castra Caesaris  5
omnibus copiis contenderunt et ab milibus passuum
minus duobus castra posuerunt; quae castra, ut fumo
atque ignibus significabatur, amplius milibus passuum
octo in latitudinem patebant.

    **8.** Caesar primo et propter multitudinem hostium et  10
propter eximiam opinionem virtutis proelio supersedere
statuit; cotidie tamen equestribus proeliis quid hostis
virtute posset et quid nostri auderent periclitabatur.
Ubi nostros non esse inferiores intellexit, loco pro castris ad aciem instruendam natura opportuno atque idoneo  15
— quod is collis, ubi castra posita erant, paululum ex
planitie editus tantum adversus in latitudinem patebat
quantum loci acies instructa occupare poterat, atque ex
utraque parte lateris deiectus habebat et in frontem
leniter fastigatus paulatim ad planitiem redibat — ab  20
utroque latere eius collis transversam fossam obduxit
circiter passuum quadringentorum et ad extremas fossas castella constituit ibique tormenta conlocavit, ne,
cum aciem instruxisset, hostes, quod tantum multitudine poterant, ab lateribus pugnantes suos circumvenire  25
possent. Hoc facto duabus legionibus quas proxime
conscripserat in castris relictis, ut, si quo opus esset,
subsidio duci possent, reliquas sex legiones pro castris
in acie constituit. Hostes item suas copias ex castris
eductas instruxerant.                                 30

    **9.** Palus erat non magna inter nostrum atque hostium
exercitum. Hanc si nostri transirent hostes exspecta-

bant; nostri autem, si ab illis initium transeundi fieret,
ut impeditos adgrederentur, parati in armis erant. Interim proelio equestri inter duas acies contendebatur. Ubi
neutri transeundi initium faciunt, secundiore equitum
5 proelio nostris Caesar suos in castra reduxit. Hostes
protinus ex eo loco ad flumen Axonam contenderunt,
quod esse post nostra castra demonstratum est. Ibi
vadis repertis partem suarum copiarum traducere conati
sunt eo consilio, ut, si possent, castellum cui praeerat
10 Q. Titurius legatus expugnarent pontemque interscinderent; si minus potuissent, agros Remorum popularentur,
qui magno nobis usui ad bellum gerendum erant, comme-
atuque nostros prohiberent.

**10.** Caesar certior factus ab Titurio omnem equitatum
15 et levis armaturae Numidas, funditores sagittariosque
pontem traducit atque ad eos contendit. Acriter in eo
loco pugnatum est. Hostes impeditos nostri in flumine adgressi magnum eorum numerum occiderunt: per
eorum corpora reliquos audacissime transire conantes
20 multitudine telorum reppulerunt; primos qui transierant
equitatu circumventos interfecerunt. Hostes, ubi et de
expugnando oppido et de flumine transeundo spem se
fefellisse intellexerunt neque nostros in locum iniqui-
orem progredi pugnandi causa viderunt, atque ipsos res
25 frumentaria deficere coepit, concilio convocato constitue-
runt optimum esse domum suam quemque reverti, et,
quorum in fines primum Romani exercitum introduxis-
sent, ad eos defendendos undique convenirent, ut potius
in suis quam in alienis finibus decertarent et domesticis
30 copiis rei frumentariae uterentur. Ad eam sententiam
cum reliquis causis haec quoque ratio eos deduxit, quod
Divitiacum atque Aeduos finibus Bellovacorum adpro-

pinquare cognoverant. His persuaderi ut diutius mora-
rentur neque suis auxilium ferrent non poterat.

**11.** Ea re constituta, secunda vigilia magno cum strepitu ac tumultu castris egressi, nullo certo ordine neque
imperio, cum sibi quisque primum itineris locum peteret 5
et domum pervenire properaret, fecerunt ut consimilis
fugae profectio videretur. Hac re statim Caesar per
speculatores cognita insidias veritus, quod qua de causa
discederent nondum perspexerat, exercitum equitatum-
que castris continuit. Prima luce confirmata re ab ex- 10
ploratoribus omnem equitatum qui novissimum agmen
moraretur praemisit. His Q. Pedium et L. Aurunculeium
Cottam legatos praefecit; T. Labienum legatum cum legionibus tribus subsequi iussit. Hi novissimos adorti et
multa milia passuum prosecuti magnam multitudinem 15
eorum fugientium conciderunt, cum ab extremo agmine
ad quos ventum erat consisterent fortiterque impetum
nostrorum militum sustinerent; priores, quod abesse a
periculo viderentur neque ulla necessitate neque imperio
continerentur, exaudito clamore perturbatis ordinibus 20
omnes in fuga sibi praesidium ponerent. Ita sine ullo
periculo tantam eorum multitudinem nostri interfecerunt quantum fuit diei spatium, sub occasumque solis
destiterunt, seque in castra, ut erat imperatum, rece-
perunt. 25

**12.** Postridie eius diei Caesar, priusquam se hostes
ex terrore ac fuga reciperent, in fines Suessionum, qui
proximi Remis erant, exercitum duxit et magno itinere
confecto ad oppidum Noviodunum contendit. Id ex
itinere oppugnare conatus, quod vacuum ab defensoribus 30
esse audiebat, propter latitudinem fossae murique altitudinem paucis defendentibus expugnare non potuit.

Castris munitis vineas agere quaeque ad oppugnandum usui erant comparare coepit. Interim omnis ex fuga Suessionum multitudo in oppidum proxima nocte con-venit. Celeriter vineis ad oppidum actis, aggere iacto 5 turribusque constitutis, magnitudine operum, quae neque viderant ante Galli neque audierant, et celeritate Roma-norum permoti, legatos ad Caesarem de deditione mittunt et petentibus Remis ut conservarentur impetrant.

**13.** Caesar obsidibus acceptis primis civitatis atque 10 ipsius Galbae regis duobus filiis, armisque omnibus ex oppido traditis, in deditionem Suessiones accepit exerci-tumque in Bellovacos ducit. Qui cum se suaque omnia in oppidum Bratuspantium contulissent, atque ab eo oppido Caesar cum exercitu circiter milia passuum quin-15 que abesset, omnes maiores natu ex oppido egressi manus ad Caesarem tendere et voce significare coeperunt sese in eius fidem ac potestatem venire neque contra populum Romanum armis contendere. Item, cum ad oppidum acces-sisset castraque ibi poneret, pueri mulieresque ex muro 20 passis manibus suo more pacem ab Romanis petierunt.

**14.** Pro his Divitiacus — nam post discessum Belga-rum dimissis Aeduorum copiis ad eum reverterat — facit verba: Bellovacos omni tempore in fide atque amicitia civitatis Aeduae fuisse: impulsos a suis principibus, qui 25 dicerent Aeduos ab Caesare in servitutem redactos omnes indignitates contumeliasque perferre, et ab Aeduis defe-cisse et populo Romano bellum intulisse. Qui eius consili principes fuissent, quod intellegerent quantam calamitatem civitati intulissent, in Britanniam profu-30 gisse. Petere non solum Bellovacos sed etiam pro his Aeduos ut sua clementia ac mansuetudine in eos uta-tur. Quod si fecerit, Aeduorum auctoritatem apud omnes

Belgas amplificaturum, quorum auxiliis atque opibus, si qua bella inciderint, sustentare consuerint.

**15.** Caesar honoris Divitiaci atque Aeduorum causa sese eos in fidem recepturum et conservaturum dixit; quod erat civitas magna inter Belgas auctoritate atque 5 hominum multitudine praestabat, sexcentos obsides poposcit. His traditis omnibusque armis ex oppido conlatis, ab eo loco in fines Ambianorum pervenit, qui se suaque omnia sine mora dediderunt. Eorum fines Nervii attingebant; quorum de natura moribusque Caesar 10 cum quaereret, sic reperiebat: Nullum aditum esse ad eos mercatoribus; nihil pati vini reliquarumque rerum inferri, quod iis rebus relanguescere animos eorum et remitti virtutem existimarent: esse homines feros magnaeque virtutis; increpitare atque incusare reliquos 15 Belgas qui se populo Romano dedidissent patriamque virtutem proiecissent; confirmare sese neque legatos missuros neque ullam condicionem pacis accepturos.

**16.** Cum per eorum fines triduum iter fecisset, inveniebat ex captivis Sabim flumen ab castris suis non 20 amplius milia passuum x abesse: trans id flumen omnes Nervios consedisse adventumque ibi Romanorum exspectare una cum Atrebatis et Veromanduis finitimis suis, nam his utrisque persuaserant uti eandem belli fortunam experirentur; exspectari etiam ab his Aduatucorum 25 copias atque esse in itinere; mulieres quique per aetatem ad pugnam inutiles viderentur in eum locum coniecisse, quo propter paludes exercitui aditus non esset.

**17.** His rebus cognitis exploratores centurionesque praemittit qui locum idoneum castris deligant. Cum ex 30 dediticiis Belgis reliquisque Gallis complures Caesarem secuti una iter facerent, quidam ex his, ut postea ex

captivis cognitum est, eorum dierum consuetudine itineris nostri exercitus perspecta, nocte ad Nervios pervene-
runt atque his demonstrarunt inter singulas legiones
impedimentorum magnum numerum intercedere, neque
5 esse quicquam negoti, cum prima legio in castra venisset, reliquaeque legiones magnum spatium abessent, hanc
sub sarcinis adoriri ; qua pulsa impedimentisque direptis
futurum ut reliquae contra consistere non auderent.
Adiuvabat etiam eorum consilium qui rem deferebant,
10 quod Nervii antiquitus, cum equitatu nihil possent
(neque enim ad hoc tempus ei rei student, sed quicquid
possunt, pedestribus valent copiis) quo facilius finiti-
morum equitatum, si praedandi causa ad eos venissent,
impedirent, teneris arboribus incisis atque inflexis, cre-
15 brisque in latitudinem ramis enatis, et rubis sentibusque
interiectis, effecerant ut instar muri hae saepes muni-
menta praeberent, quo non modo non intrari sed ne
perspici quidem posset.   His rebus cum iter agminis
nostri impediretur, non omittendum sibi consilium Nervii
20 existimaverunt.

**18.** Loci natura erat haec, quem locum nostri castris
delegerant.   Collis ab summo aequaliter declivis ad flumen Sabim, quod supra nominavimus, vergebat.   Ab eo
flumine pari adclivitate collis nascebatur adversus huic
25 et contrarius, passus circiter ducentos infimus apertus,
ab superiore parte silvestris ut non facile introrsus perspici posset.   Intra eas silvas hostes in occulto sese
continebant ; in aperto loco secundum flumen paucae
stationes equitum videbantur.   Fluminis erat altitudo
30 pedum circiter trium.

**19.** Caesar equitatu praemisso subsequebatur omnibus
copiis ; sed ratio ordoque agminis aliter se habebat ac

Belgae ad Nervios detulerant. Nam quod ad hostes adpropinquabat, consuetudine sua Caesar sex legiones expeditas ducebat; post eas totius exercitus impedimenta conlocarat; inde duae legiones quae proxime conscriptae erant totum agmen claudebant praesidioque impedimentis 5 erant. Equites nostri, cum funditoribus sagittariisque flumen transgressi, cum hostium equitatu proelium commiserunt. Cum se illi identidem in silvas ad suos reci perent ac rursus ex silva in nostros impetum facerent, neque nostri longius quam quem ad finem porrecta loca 10 aperta pertinebant cedentes insequi auderent, interim legiones sex, quae primae venerant, opere dimenso castra munire coeperunt. Ubi prima impedimenta nostri exercitus ab iis qui in silvis abditi latebant visa sunt, quod tempus inter eos committendi proeli convenerat, ut intra 15 silvas aciem ordinesque constituerant atque ipsi sese confirmaverant, subito omnibus copiis provolaverunt impetumque in nostros equites fecerunt. His facile pulsis ac proturbatis, incredibili celeritate ad flumen decucurrerunt, ut paene uno tempore et ad silvas et in flumine 20 et iam in manibus nostris hostes viderentur. Eadem autem celeritate adverso colle ad nostra castra atque eos qui in opere occupati erant contenderunt.

**20.** Caesari omnia uno tempore erant agenda: vexillum proponendum, quod erat insigne cum ad arma con- 25 curri oporteret, signum tuba dandum, ab opere revocandi milites, qui paulo longius aggeris petendi causa processerant arcessendi, acies instruenda, milites cohortandi, signum dandum. Quarum rerum magnam partem temporis brevitas et successus hostium impediebat. His 30 difficultatibus duae res erant subsidio — scientia atque usus militum, quod superioribus proeliis exercitati, quid

fieri oporteret non minus commode ipsi sibi praescribere
quam ab aliis doceri poterant; et quod ab opere singu-
lisque legionibus singulos legatos Caesar discedere nisi
munitis castris vetuerat.  Hi propter propinquitatem et
5 celeritatem hostium nihil iam Caesaris imperium exspec-
tabant, sed per se quae videbantur administrabant.

**21.** Caesar necessariis rebus imperatis ad cohortandos
milites quam in partem fors obtulit decucurrit et ad
legionem decimam devenit.  Milites non longiore ora-
10 tione cohortatus quam uti suae pristinae virtutis memoriam retinerent neu perturbarentur animo hostiumque
impetum fortiter sustinerent, quod non longius hostes
aberant quam quo telum adici posset, proeli committendi
signum dedit.  Atque in alteram partem item cohortandi
15 causa profectus pugnantibus occurrit.  Temporis tanta
fuit exiguitas hostiumque tam paratus ad dimicandum
animus, ut non modo ad insignia adcommodanda, sed
etiam ad galeas induendas scutisque tegimenta detru-
denda tempus defuerit.  Quam quisque ab opere in par-
20 tem casu devenit quaeque prima signa conspexit, ad
haec constitit, ne in quaerendis suis pugnandi tempus
dimitteret.

**22.** Instructo exercitu magis ut loci natura deiectus-
que collis et necessitas temporis quam ut rei militaris
25 ratio atque ordo postulabat, cum diversis legionibus aliae
alia in parte hostibus resisterent, saepibusque densis-
simis, ut ante demonstravimus, interiectis prospectus
impediretur, neque certa subsidia conlocari, neque quid
in quaque parte opus esset provideri, neque ab uno
30 omnia imperia administrari poterant.  Itaque in tanta
rerum iniquitate, fortunae quoque eventus varii seque-
bantur.

**23.** Legionis nonae et decimae milites, ut in sinistra parte acie constiterant, pilis emissis, cursu ac lassitudine exanimatos vulneribusque confectos Atrebates — nam his ea pars obvenerat — celeriter ex loco superiore in flumen compulerunt et transire conantes insecuti gladiis 5 magnam partem eorum impeditam interfecerunt. Ipsi transire flumen non dubitaverunt, et in locum iniquum progressi, rursus resistentes hostes redintegrato proelio in fugam coniecerunt. Item alia in parte diversae duae legiones, undecima et octava, profligatis Veromanduis, 10 quibuscum erant congressi, ex loco superiore in ipsis fluminis ripis proeliabantur. At totis fere a fronte et ab sinistra parte nudatis castris, cum in dextro cornu legio duodecima et non magno ab ea intervallo septima constitisset, omnes Nervii confertissimo agmine duce 15 Boduognato qui summam imperi tenebat, ad eum locum contenderunt; quorum pars aperto latere legiones circumvenire, pars summum castrorum locum petere coepit.

**24.** Eodem tempore equites nostri levisque armaturae pedites, qui cum iis una fuerant, quos primo hostium 20 impetu pulsos dixeram, cum se in castra reciperent, adversis hostibus occurrebant ac rursus aliam in partem fugam petebant; et calones, qui ab decumana porta ac summo iugo collis nostros victores flumen transisse conspexerant, praedandi causa egressi, cum respexissent et 25 hostes in nostris castris versari vidissent, praecipites fugae sese mandabant. Simul eorum qui cum impedimentis veniebant clamor fremitusque oriebatur, aliique aliam in partem perterriti ferebantur. Quibus omnibus rebus permoti equites Treveri, quorum inter Gallos virtutis 30 opinio est singularis, qui auxili causa ab civitate ad Caesarem missi venerant, cum multitudine hostium

castra compleri, legiones premi et paene circumventas
teneri, calones, equites, funditores, Numidas, diversos
dissipatosque in omnes partes fugere vidissent, despera-
tis nostris rebus domum contenderunt; Romanos pulsos
5 superatosque, castris impedimentisque eorum hostes po-
titos civitati renuntiaverunt.

**25.** Caesar ab decimae legionis cohortatione ad dex
trum cornu profectus, ubi suos urgeri signisque in unum
locum conlatis duodecimae legionis confertos milites sibi
10 ipsos ad pugnam esse impedimento vidit — quartae
cohortis omnibus centurionibus occisis signiferoque interfecto, signo amisso, reliquarum cohortium omnibus
fere centurionibus aut vulneratis aut occisis, in his pri-
mipilo P. Sextio Baculo, fortissimo viro, multis gravi-
15 busque vulneribus confecto ut iam se sustinere non
posset, reliquos esse tardiores, et nonnullos ab novissimis deserto proelio excedere ac tela vitare, hostes neque
a fronte ex inferiore loco subeuntes intermittere et ab
utroque latere instare, et rem esse in angusto vidit,
20 neque ullum esse subsidium quod submitti posset —
scuto ab novissimis uni militi detracto, quod ipse eo sine
scuto venerat, in primam aciem processit centurioni-
busque nominatim appellatis reliquos cohortatus milites
signa inferre et manipulos laxare iussit, quo facilius
25 gladiis uti possent. Cuius adventu spe inlata militibus
ac redintegrato animo, cum pro se quisque in conspectu
imperatoris etiam in extremis suis rebus operam navare
cuperet, paulum hostium impetus tardatus est.

**26.** Caesar cum septimam legionem, quae iuxta con-
30 stiterat, item urgeri ab hoste vidisset, tribunos militum
monuit ut paulatim sese legiones coniungerent et conversa signa in hostes inferrent. Quo facto, cum alius

alii subsidium ferret, neque timerent ne aversi ab hoste
circumvenirentur, audacius resistere ac fortius pugnare
coeperunt. Interim milites legionum duarum, quae in
novissimo agmine praesidio impedimentis fuerant, proelio
nuntiato cursu incitato in summo colle ab hostibus con- 5
spiciebantur; et T. Labienus castris hostium potitus et
ex loco superiore quae res in nostris castris gererentur
conspicatus decimam legionem subsidio nostris misit.
Qui cum ex equitum et calonum fuga, quo in loco res
esset, quantoque in periculo et castra et legiones et 10
imperator versaretur, cognovissent, nihil ad celeritatem
sibi reliqui fecerunt.

**27.** Horum adventu tanta rerum commutatio est facta
ut nostri, etiam qui vulneribus confecti procubuissent,
scutis innixi proelium redintegrarent; tum calones per- 15
territos hostes conspicati etiam inermes armatis occur-
rerent; equites vero, ut turpitudinem fugae virtute
delerent, omnibus in locis pugnae se legionariis militibus praeferrent. At hostes etiam in extrema spe salutis
tantam virtutem praestiterunt ut, cum primi eorum 20
cecidissent, proximi iacentibus insisterent atque ex
eorum corporibus pugnarent; his deiectis et coacer-
vatis cadaveribus, qui superessent ut ex tumulo tela in
nostros conicerent et pila intercepta remitterent: ut non
nequiquam tantae virtutis homines iudicari deberet ausos 25
esse transire latissimum flumen, ascendere altissimas
ripas, subire iniquissimum locum; quae facilia ex difficillimis animi magnitudo redegerat.

**28.** Hoc proelio facto et prope ad internecionem gente
ac nomine Nerviorum redacto maiores natu, quos una 30
cum pueris mulieribusque in aestuaria ac paludes coniec-
tos dixeramus, hac pugna nuntiata, cum victoribus nihil

impeditum, victis nihil tutum arbitrarentur, omnium qui
supererant consensu legatos ad Caesarem miserunt seque
ei dediderunt; et in commemoranda civitatis calamitate
ex sexcentis ad tres senatores, ex hominum milibus LX
5 vix ad quingentos qui arma ferre possent sese redactos
esse dixerunt. Quos Caesar, ut in miseros ac supplices
usus misericordia videretur, diligentissime conservavit
suisque finibus atque oppidis uti iussit, et finitimis im-
peravit ut ab iniuria et maleficio se suosque prohiberent.
10 **29.** Aduatuci, de quibus supra scripsimus, cum omnibus copiis auxilio Nerviis venirent, hac pugna nuntiata
ex itinere domum reverterunt; cunctis oppidis castellis-
que desertis sua omnia in unum oppidum egregie natura
munitum contulerunt. Quod cum ex omnibus in circuitu
15 partibus altissimas rupes despectusque haberet, una ex
parte leniter adclivis aditus in latitudinem non amplius
ducentorum pedum relinquebatur; quem locum duplici
altissimo muro munierant, tum magni ponderis saxa et
praeacutas trabes in muro conlocabant. Ipsi erant ex
20 Cimbris Teutonisque prognati, qui, cum iter in provin-
ciam nostram atque Italiam facerent, iis impedimentis,
quae secum agere ac portare non poterant, citra flumen
Rhenum depositis custodiam ex suis ac praesidium sex
milia hominum una reliquerunt. Hi post eorum obitum
25 multos annos a finitimis exagitati, cum alias bellum
inferrent, alias inlatum defenderent, consensu eorum
omnium pace facta hunc sibi domicilio locum delegerunt.
    **30.**. Ac primo adventu exercitus nostri crebras ex
oppido excursiones faciebant parvulisque proeliis cum
30 nostris contendebant; postea vallo pedum XII in circuitu
XV milium crebrisque castellis circummuniti oppido sese
continebant. Ubi vineis actis aggere exstructo turrim

procul constitui viderunt, primum inridere ex muro atque
increpitare vocibus, quod tanta machinatio ab tanto spatio
instrueretur : quibusnam manibus aut quibus viribus
praesertim homines tantulae staturae — nam plerumque
hominibus Gallis prae magnitudine corporum suorum 5
brevitas nostra contemptui est — tanti oneris turrim in
muro sese conlocare confiderent ?

**31.** Ubi vero moveri et adpropinquare moenibus viderunt, nova atque inusitata specie commoti legatos ad
Caesarem de pace miserunt, qui ad hunc modum locuti : 10
'Non existimare Romanos sine ope divina bellum gerere,
qui tantae altitudinis machinationes tanta celeritate pro-
movere possent ; se suaque omnia eorum potestati permittere' dixerunt. 'Unum petere ac deprecari : si forte
pro sua clementia ac mansuetudine, quam ipsi ab aliis 15
audirent, statuisset Aduatucos esse conservandos, ne se
armis despoliaret. Sibi omnes fere finitimos esse in-
imicos ac suae virtuti invidere ; a quibus se defendere
traditis armis non possent. Sibi praestare, si in eum
casum deducerentur, quamvis fortunam a populo Romano 20
pati, quam ab his per cruciatum interfici, inter quos
dominari consuessent.'

**32.** Ad haec Caesar respondit : 'Se magis consuetudine sua quam merito eorum civitatem conservaturum, si
prius quam murum aries attigisset se dedidissent ; sed 25
deditionis nullam esse condicionem nisi armis traditis.
Se id quod in Nerviis fecisset facturum finitimisque
imperaturum, ne quam dediticiis populi Romani iniuriam
inferrent.' Re nuntiata ad suos, quae imperarentur
facere dixerunt. Armorum magna multitudine de muro 30
in fossam quae erat ante oppidum iacta sic ut prope
summam muri aggerisque altitudinem acervi armorum

adaequarent, et tamen circiter parte tertia, ut postea perspectum est, celata atque in oppido retenta, portis patefactis eo die pace sunt usi.

**33.** Sub vesperum Caesar portas claudi militesque ex
5 oppido exire iussit, ne quam noctu oppidani ab militibus iniuriam acciperent. Illi ante inito, ut intellectum est, consilio, quod deditione facta nostros praesidia deducturos aut denique indiligentius servaturos crediderant — partim cum iis quae retinuerant et celaverant armis,
10 partim scutis ex cortice factis aut viminibus intextis, quae subito, ut temporis exiguitas postulabat, pellibus induxerant — tertia vigilia, qua minime arduus ad nostras munitiones ascensus videbatur, omnibus copiis repentino ex oppido eruptionem fecerunt. Celeriter, ut ante Cae-
15 sar imperarat, ignibus significatione facta ex proximis castellis eo concursum est, pugnatumque ab hostibus ita acriter est ut a viris fortibus in extrema spe salutis iniquo loco contra eos qui ex vallo turribusque tela iacerent pugnari debuit, cum in una virtute omnis spes
20 salutis consisteret. Occisis ad hominum milibus quattuor reliqui in oppidum reiecti sunt. Postridie eius diei refractis portis, cum iam defenderet nemo, atque intromissis militibus nostris sectionem eius oppidi universam Caesar vendidit. Ab iis qui emerant capitum numerus
25 ad eum relatus est milium quinquaginta trium.

**34.** Eodem tempore a P. Crasso, quem cum legione una miserat ad Venetos, Unellos, Osismos, Curiosolitas, Esuvios, Aulercos, Redones, quae sunt maritimae civitates Oceanumque attingunt, certior factus est omnes
30 eas civitates in dicionem potestatemque populi Romani esse redactas.

**35.** His rebus gestis omni Gallia pacata, tanta huius belli ad barbaros opinio perlata est uti ab iis nationibus, quae trans Rhenum incolerent mitterentur legati ad Caesarem, qui se obsides daturas, imperata facturas pollicerentur. Quas legationes Caesar, quod in Italiam Illyri- 5 cumque properabat, inita proxima aestate ad se reverti iussit. Ipse in Carnutes, Andes Turonesque, quae civitates propinquae his locis erant ubi bellum gesserat, legionibus in hibernacula deductis, in Italiam profectus est. Ob easque res ex litteris Caesaris dies quindecim 10 supplicatio decreta est, quod ante id tempus accidit nulli.

# NOTES.

INTRODUCTORY NOTE. —To translate Latin into English is to express the meaning of the Latin in English words and in the English idiom. But the meaning must be discovered before it can be expressed. Discovering the sense is, therefore, a process preparatory to translation, but yet measurably distinct from it. For discovering the meaning, the golden rule is, *Take words and clauses in the order in which they stand.* If the first chapter of this book were rendered into English words exactly in the Latin order, the thought would be readily apprehended by any one quite unacquainted with Latin. Such a word for word rendering, mental or oral, is for the beginner a necessary preliminary to translation, but, I repeat, must not be confounded with translation. For that, the golden rule is, *Express the thought in pure English, without admixture of Latin idiom.*

---

Notes under the heading CHAP. refer to the simplified text ; those that follow, under the heading PAGE, supplement the former and refer to the unchanged text. The grammatical references are to the Latin Grammars of Allen and Greenough, Bennett (B.), Harkness (H.), and Hale and Buck (H-B.). References in parentheses are to the old editions.

CHAP. 1,

line 2. **certior fiēbat** : *he was made more certain = he was informed.* **fiēbat** : the passive of **facio.** Review the forms. 204 (142) ; B. 131 ; H. 296 (294) ; H-B. 195.

4. **Coniūrandi** : pronounce the *i* of the second syllable like *y.*

5. **verēbantur** : the subject is **Belgae,** understood ; supply the same subject for **sollicitābantur.**

**ad se** : refers to the subject of **verēbantur.**

6. **Germānos** : subject-accusative of **versāri** ; *that the Germans should remain.*

8. **exercitum** : subject-accusative of **hiemāre** and **inveterāscere.**

**inveterāscere** : *get a foothold;* but what is its primary meaning from its derivation ?

43

line 10. **imperiis** : 368, 3 (227, e, 3) ; B. 127, II ; H. 426, 1 (385) ; H-B. 363, footnote 3, b.

11. **iis** : supply mentally **ab** before it.

13. **qui** : *and these,* referring to **potentiōres,** etc.

**eam rem** : read again the preceding sentence, and you will see to what **eam rem** refers.

**imperio nostro** : *under our* (i.e. Roman) *rule.* The ablative implies condition, and the meaning is, *if we should get the sovereignty.* 420, 4 (255, d, 4) ; B. 227, 2, b ; H. 489, 1 (431, 2, (3)) ; H-B. 421, 6.

PAGE **23,**

1. **ita uti**: *as.*

3. **Labiēni** : Cæsar's lieutenant was now in the country of the Sequani. See a map of **Gallia.**

4. **quam**: *whose country.* We might expect **quos** referring to **Belgas,** but the relative is made to agree with the predicate noun **partem.**

6. **has esse causas** : depending on **rūmōres adferēbantur,** like **Belgas ... coniūrāre** and **obsides ... dare.** 459 (272); B. 331, I ; H. 613 (535) ; H-B. 589.

7. **omni ... Gallia** : all except their country.

**pācāta** : the Romans, with cruel humor, called a country " pacified " when they had enslaved it.

8. **partim qui** : *some of whom.*

9. **ut ... ita** : *as ... so.*

11. **partim qui** : *others of whom.*

12. **ab nōnnūllis etiam** : these, then, are the third class by whom it is said, **Belgae sollicitābantur** : first, the conservative and patriotic ; second, the restless and dissatisfied; third, the selfish and ambitious.

CHAP. **2,**

2. **interiōrem Galliam** : *the interior of Gaul ;* that is, Gaul beyond the Alps. Refer constantly to a map.

3. **qui ... dēdūceret** : **qui** refers to **Q. Pedium,** and the clause **qui ... dēdūceret** denotes purpose, *to lead.*

4. **Ipse** : supply **Caesar.**

6. **Ea** = **eas res,** as shown by **rēbus** following.

8. **manus cōgi** : *that parties of men were gathering.* The construction is the same as **Belgas ... coniūrāre,** in chap. 1.

9. **condūci**: *was mustering ;* a very different meaning in chap. 1.

**quīn ... proficīscerētur** : *to march.* What literally ?

**PAGE 23,**

line 18. **inita aestāte**: *when summer had begun* = *at the beginning of summer;* marks the time of **dēdūceret**, not of **mīsit.**

**PAGE 24,**

1. **Dat negōtium**: *he charges.* What literally?

2. **utī** (same as **ut**) . . . **cōgnōscant**: *to find out;* the clause depends on **dat negōtium.**

3. **se**: refers to Caesar.

**certiōrem faciant**: compare the passive form in chap. 1.

5. **dubitandum**: in full the sentence would be, **Caesar dubitandum esse sibi nōn exīstimāvit**; and the word for word rendering, *Cæsar did not think an-obligation-of-hesitating to be to himself.* Translate, *he ought to hesitate.*

**CHAP. 3,**

1. **Eo**: that is, **ad fīnes Belgārum.** See the end of chap. 2.

3. **se** . . . **permittere**: here **se** is the subject-accusative of **permittere.**

**in fidem**: *to the protection.*

6. **Caesaris imperāta facere**: *to do what Cæsar required.* Literally what?

7. **oppidīs recipere**: in meaning = **in oppida recipere.**

**cēteris**: not *other*, but *all other.* Their submission is abject.

9. **sēse**: not different from **se.**

10. **Suessiōnes**: the object of **dēterrēre.**

12. **iūre**: *constitution.*

**īsdem**: oftener written **iīsdem**, 101, c.

**PAGE 24,**

9. **omni opīniōne**: *than any one could expect.* 406, a (247, b) ; B. 217, 4 ; H. 471 (417) ; H–B. 416, e.

10. **ex Belgis** = **Belgārum**, or **inter Belgas.**

12. **qui dīcerent**: compare **qui dēdūceret**, p. 23, l. 19, and note on simplified text.

**se**: the object (with **sua omnia** = *their all*) of **permittere.** Another **se** must be mentally supplied as the subject of **permittere.**

18. **incolant**: why not **incolunt**, for it must be translated as if it were **incolunt**? Because the clause **qui . . . incolant** depends on the clause **Germānos . . . coniūnxisse.**

It is therefore *a dependent clause of indirect discourse*, and as such must have the subjunctive. Thoroughly master this, the most important principle of Latin syntax. Mark how the descriptive clause, **qui . . . incolant**, *is framed into* the main clause.

line 19. **furōrem**: the politic or cowardly Remi considered the love of liberty and independence of their brother Belgæ *blind passion*.

20. **qui . . . ûtantur**: *though they . . . enjoyed.* **qui**, then, must sometimes be rendered *though he*, *though they*, etc., but only when the subjunctive follows.

21. **ûtantur**: supply immediately following **atque**.

22. **ipsis**: refers to **Rēmi**.

23. **quin . . . cōnsentīrent**: *from . . . uniting.* Compare **quin . . . proficīscerētur**, p. 24, l. 6, and note on simplified text.

CHAP. **4**,

1. **quantae**: refers to extent of country and population.

  **in armis essent**: connect with **quae cīvitātes**: *what states were in arms, and how powerful they were.*

2. **quid in bello possent**: a literal translation, *what they could* (do) *in war*, does not convey the meaning. Render, *what force they could bring into the field.*

4. **ibi**: **cis Rhēnum**.

6. **ex re**: equivalent to **ex causa**.

7. **fiēbat**: *it was coming about.* The Remi said, in direct discourse, **fit**; and below, **sūmant**.

  **spīritus**: means in the singular *air*, and is here used just as we use "airs," in the phrase "to put on airs."

8. **omnia . . . explōrāta**: *full information.*

9. **Quantam quisque**: notice the order. **Quisque** likes to stand after **quantus**, **quotus**, **se**, and **suus**; here it means *each nation.*

11. **Plūrimum . . . valēbant**: about equivalent to **plūrimum poterant**, *had the most power.*

18. **cum . . . tum**: *not only . . . but also.*

19. **Britanniae**: "the first mention of Britain by a Roman author."

PAGE **24,**

line 27. **propter fertilitātem**: to be connected with **cōnsēdisse.**

28. **incolerent**: why not **incolēbant**? See note on p. 24, l. 18, **qui . . . incolant.**

29. **memoria**: *within the memory;* but two lines below, *because of the memory.*

PAGE **25,**

10. **nostra etiam memoria**: compare **patrum nostrōrum memoria**, p. 24, l. 29.

13. **obtinuerit**: *held,* not *obtained,* which is usually expressed by **adsecūtus est, cōnsecūtus est,** or **adeptus est.**

15. **omnium voluntāte**: *with the assent of all.*

23. **arbitrāri**: that is, **Rēmos arbitrāri.**

CHAP. **5,**

2. **obsides**: *as hostages,* in apposition with **līberos.** What would have been the fate of these, if the chieftains had broken their pledges?

4. **Rēi pūblicae interest**: *it concerns the* (Roman) *republic.* The real subject of **interest,** represented in English by *it,* is **manus hostium distinēri.**

**manus**: the subject-accusative of **distinēri,** *to be kept from uniting.*

5. **ne . . . cōnflīgendum sit**: *that it may not be necessary to fight.*

7. **intrōdūxerint**: the Roman way of speaking is: this can be done, if that *shall be done, or shall have been done;* hence the future perfect. But mark that such a future or future perfect is often best rendered by a present.

9. **coāctas . . . venīre**: *having been assembled . . . to be coming* = *had assembled . . . and were coming.*

10. **vīdit** = **intellēxit.**

**neque iam** = **et iam nōn.**

**iis**: take with **explōrātōribus.**

13. **quae res**: that is, his crossing the river and fixing his camp there.

14. **post eum quae essent** = **ea quae post eum essent,** *his rear.* What should you expect in place of **eum**?

**tūta**: goes with the whole expression, **post eum quae essent.**

line 16. **portāri** : *be brought down the river to him.*
　19. **in altitūdinem** : *to the height.*
　20. **duodēvīginti pedum** : that is, **in lātitūdinem**, *in width.*

PAGE 25,

24. **līberāliterque ōrātiōne prōsecūtus** : **līberāliter** means *in a generous or kindly manner;* **ōrātiōne** indicates in what sense **prōsecūtus** is to be taken, *accompanying with words;* finally, **prōsequor** has its common meaning of *accompany,* but with the meaning unusually applied : Cæsar had encouraged the Remi, and he *accompanies the encouragement with kind words.* Translate, *Cæsar encouraging the Remi and adding kind words.*

29. **commūnis salūtis** : by the *common interests* Cæsar means those of the Ædui and the Romans.

30. **cōnflīgendum sit** : compare **dubitandum (esse)** p. 24, l. 5, and read the note. Here, as there, **sibi**, referring to Cæsar and the Ædui, must be mentally supplied, showing for whom the duty or necessity of action (hesitating, fighting) exists.

31. **Id fieri posse** : depends upon **docet.** To what does **id** refer ?

PAGE 26,

1. **Postquam . . . vīdit . . . cōgnōvit, . . . mātūrāvit** : *when he saw . . . and found out,* (then) *. . . he hastened.*

3. **neque . . . cōgnōvit** : *and from those scouts,* etc., *found out that they* (the Belgæ) *were now not far distant.*

8. **et** connects **reddēbat** and **efficiēbat**, which have the same subject, **quae res.** The order makes this sentence difficult. Cæsar might have written : **et efficiēbat ut commeātus ab Rēmis reliquīsque cīvitātibus sine perīculo ad eum portāri posset.** The order is so perplexed and perplexing because Cæsar wrote in haste, and because he began with the word which was uppermost in his mind, **commeātus.**

CHAP. 6,

2. **ex itinere** : *immediately after their march.*
3. **sustentātum est** : *the Remi held out.* What literally ?

line 4. **Gallōrum ... oppūgnātio** : *the mode of attacking towns common to the Gauls and Belgœ.*

5. **tōtis moenibus** : dative, though by some thought to ·be an ablative, *all around the walls.* 370 (228) ; B. 187, III ; H. 429, 2 (386, 2); H–B. 376.

7. **testūdine facta** : *forming a testudo.* What the soldiers did was to lap their shields over their heads.

8. **cum** : *since.* What mode follows **cum** in this sense ? ·

11. **nūntium ... mittit** : one of the expressions that are followed by the accusative and infinitive ; here, **sēse ... posse.** Compare in chapter 1, **certior flēbat,** followed by **Belgas ... coniūrāre** ; in chap. 4, **reperiēbat,** followed by **Belgas ortos esse,** in complete text.

**Iccius Rēmus** : *Iccius, a Remian.*

13. **sēse** : subject-accusative of **posse.**

PAGE 26,

19. **moenibus ... mūrum ... mūrus ... mūrum** : Cæsar's haste in writing is often manifest.

20. **coepti sunt** : it may seem strange that the passive should be used instead of the active, **coepērunt** ; but see 143, a ; H. 297, 1.

22. **Quod** : how is a relative after a period often best rendered ? For an example, see note on **qui,** chap. 1, l. 13, simplified text.

24. **nūlli** : mark the emphasis from the position. Many similar cases occur, notwithstanding A. & G., 597, b (p. 389, Rem.).

**oppūgnandi** = **oppūgnātiōnis.**

25. **summa nōbilitāte et grātia** : a descriptive ablative ; *a man of the highest rank and popularity.*

26. **praefuerat** : render as if an imperfect. The meaning is, he had been placed in command and was then in command.

**ex iis** : the same as **eōrum.**

27. **lēgāti** : *as envoys.* Compare the use of **obsides** as an appositive, p. 25, l. 26.

28. **submittātur** : can you make out the force of the **sub** ?

CHAP. 7,

2. **subsidio oppidānis** : *to aid the people in the town.* But what literally ? For the construction, see 382, 1, N. 1 • (233, a) ; B. 191, 2 ; H. 433 (390) ; H–B. 360, a, b.

line 3. **quōrum adventu** : *in consequence of their coming.*

5. **contendērunt**: the subject is **hostes**, suggested by **hosti-bus** in the preceding sentence.

6. **ab**: *distant, off, away ;* so used chiefly with numerals.

**ab mīlibus passuum minus duōbus**: a word for word rendering would be, *distant thousands of paces less than two ;* that is, *less than two miles distant.*

**PAGE 26,**

3. **neque . . . cōgnōvit**: *and learned from those scouts whom he had sent and from the Remi that they were now not far distant.*

30. **isdem ducibus**: *the same persons as guides.* Compare **qui lēgāti,** p. 26, l. 27, and note on simplified text.

**PAGE 27,**

3. **apud oppidum**: **ad** is more usual.

4. **agros . . . dēpopulāti — vīcis aedificiīsque . . . incēn-sis**: literally, *having laid waste the fields — the villages and buildings having been burned.* Mark how the construction changes for want of a deponent verb in place of **incendo**.

9. **in lātitūdinem**: compare **in altitūdinem,** p. 26, l. 13.

**CHAP. 8,**

2. **eximiam . . . virtūtis**: *their eminent reputation for valor.*

3. **quid virtūte posset**: *what their real eminence in valor was* Compare **quid in bello possent,** chap. 4, l. 2.

7. **tantum . . . patēbat quantum loci**: render *as if loci* depended on **tantum** instead of **quantum,** *extended over as much space as.*

**adversus**: *facing the enemy ;* **adversus** an adjective, agree-ing with **collis**.

**in lātitūdinem**: *laterally.* Compare chap 7, l. 8.

8. **ex utrāque parte lateris = ex utrōque latere**: *on,* not *from, both sides ;* so **ab,** below, l. 10.

10. **ad plānitiem redībat**: *gradually resumed* (impf.) *a level.* Cæsar describes a hill over against the enemy, having steep sides, and a front only broad enough for his army when arranged for battle. In front the hill rose with a gentle ascent, and at the top blended with the plain. It is possible that **lēniter fastīgātus** means, as the dic-

tionaries define on this passage and as many editors say, *gently sloping down;* in which case, **ad plānitiem redībat** would mean *sank down gradually to the level at its base.* This attributes an improbable meaning to **fastīgātus.**

line 12. **extrēmas fossas**: *at the ends of the trenches;* compare in chap. 2, l. 2, **interiōrem Galliam,** *the interior of Gaul.* **castella**: there were, then, four.

17. **ēductas īnstrūxerant**: to make good English, render as if **ēductas** were a verb followed by **et**; so, very often, when a perfect participle and verb are closely connected.

PAGE **27,**

10. **et . . . et**: we do not say *both . . . and* so frequently as we find **et . . . et** in Latin; accordingly it will generally be found better to omit in translation the first **et,** and render the second *and* *also.*

11. **proelio . . . proeliis**: *a decisive battle . . . skirmishes.*

14. **loco**: ablative absolute, *as there was a place.*

21. **obdūxit**: Cæsar elsewhere commonly uses **perdūco** of running a wall or trench. Why **obdūco** here? Because the **fossae** were dug *against* the enemy, or to *cover his position.*

24. **cum . . . īnstrūxisset**: Cæsar's thought was, according to Latin idiom, *when I shall have drawn up,* **īnstrūxero**; but such a future perfect of direct speech becomes pluperfect subjunctive in narration, after a past tense in the principal clause.

24. **quod . . . poterant**: *because they were so strong in numbers.* Find two other similar uses of **possum.**

27. **si quo opus esset**: *if there should be need of them anywhere;* not, *if there should be need of any thing.*

28. **subsidio**: in meaning and construction like **subsidio,** p. 26, l. 32.

CHAP. **9,**

2. **si . . . trānsīrent**: *to see if our men would cross this* (**hanc**).

3. **contendēbātur**: *there was fighting.* Compare chap. 6, l. 3, **sustentātum est.**

4. **neutri**: *neither of the two armies.*

5. **secundiōre . . . nostris**: *as the cavalry skirmish proved rather favorable to our men.*

line 9. **castellum**: read over again the last half of chap. 5.
Cæsar makes no mention there of a **castellum**.

10. **potuissent**: the thought was, according to the Latin idiom,
"if we shall not have been able" (**potuerimus**); but
such a future perfect of direct speech becomes a pluperfect subjunctive in narration after a past tense.

**PAGE 28,**

1. **nostri autem**, etc.: a difficult sentence; but treat it as
directed in the Introductory Note, p. 43, only observing
that **si** has its usual meaning of *if*, and **impeditos**, *when
they should get stuck fast*, agrees with **hostes** understood.

2. **ut . . . adgrederentur**: expresses the purpose of **parati
in armis erant**.

9. **eo consilio**: *with this design;* explained by **ut castellum
. . . expugnarent**.

**possent**: they said to themselves, *if we shall be able*, **pote-
rimus**; *but if we shall not have succeeded*, **si minus potuerimus**; hence **potuissent**, when related. See note on
**Instruxisset**, p. 27, l. 24.

12. **nobis usui**: compare **subsidio oppidanis**, p. 26, l. 32.

**CHAP. 10,**

3. **pugnatum est**: contains its own subject, *there was fierçe
fighting.* See **contendebatur**, chap. 9, l. 3, and note.

4. **impeditos**: *while they were struggling.*

6. **circumventos interfecerunt**: *they surrounded and killed.*
Read again the note on **eductas Instruxerant**, chap. 8,
l. 17.

7. **spem**: subject-accusative of **fefellisse**; but translate, *that
they were disappointed in the hope.*

**neque**: take the negative part with **progredi**.

8. **ipsos**: that is, **se ipsos**, namely, **hostes**.

10. **quemque**: subject-accusative of **reverti**. See also note on
chap. 4, l. 9.

11. **quorum . . . ad eos**: you will very often find the relative
clause preceding the antecedent. In almost all such cases
the English way of speaking requires us to render the
antecedent clause first.

line 13. **Quod**: *this,* referring to the last two sentences.

**eo cōnsilio** : *with this design,* explained by the following clause.

16. **Hīs persuādērī** : depends on **nōn poterat.** Why did not Cæsar write, **Hī persuādērī** ... **nōn poterant,** since he means, *these could not be persuaded ?* 372 (230) ; B. 187, II, b ; H. 302, 6 (301, 1) ; H–B. 364, 2, 292, a.

PAGE **28,**

19. **reliquos . . . cōnantes**: *the rest . . . while they were trying.*

21. **Hostes** : subject of **cōnstituērunt,** l. 25, while a pronoun referring to **hostes** may be mentally supplied as subject of **intellēxērunt** and **vīdērunt.** This sentence illustrates an important principle of Latin order, attention to which will be of great aid in translation. When the verb of the principal clause and that of the dependent clause have the same subject, it is commonly expressed in the principal, and left out in the dependent, clause. In English we do the opposite. We often begin with the dependent clause; the Latin *frames it into* the principal clause.

21. **ubi**: repeat mentally with **vīdērunt** and **coepit.**

28. **ad eos dēfendendos** : illustrates a very common way of expressing a purpose.

CHAP. **11,**

1. **ea re** : that is, to disperse to their homes ; chap. 10, l. 10.

2. **ēgressi** : the subject is **Belgae,** understood.

3. **cōnsimilis** : *altogether like.* What is the force of **con** ?

4. **Caesar** : as the subject of **veritus** and **continuit, Caesar** seems strangely placed in the grip of the ablative absolute; but the position shows by whom the knowledge was got. *Caesar getting wind of this movement immediately through his spies.*

5. **veritus** : try always to render a participle so as to show its logical relation to the main verb, whether of time, cause, contrast, or what not ; here, *because he feared.*

**castris** : substantially equivalent to **in castris.**

6. **qui ... morārētur** : compare **qui dēdūceret,** chap. 2, l. 3, and note.

line 10. **ventum erat**: *they had come.* Compare **sustentātum est,** chap. 6, l. 3 ; **contendēbātur,** chap. 9, l. 3.

11. **priōres**: *those in advance.*

15. **sub**: *towards.* The idea of *place* being transferred to that of *time.*

**PAGE 29,**

5. **quisque**: see p. 25, l. 3, and note on simplified text.

**prīmum itineris locum**: *the first place on the road.*

8. **qua . . . discēderent**: following **quod . . . perspēxerat.**

16. **cum . . . cōnsisterent**: *since the enemy, at the very extremity of the rear, kept making a stand.*

18. **priōres**: **et** understood ; *while those in advance.*

**quod**: carry on also into the next clause ; *and because they were not held together* (**continērentur**).

21. **sine ūllo perīculo**: two ways of expressing "without any" in this chapter ; for above we have **nūllo certo ōrdine,** *without any definite order.*

23. **quantum . . . spatium**: *how great a space of time* (**diēi**) *there was ;* that is (they killed as great a number) *as the length of the time allowed.*

24. **sēque in castra . . . recēpērunt**: *and they and their pitiless commander probably slept well that night.*

**CHAP. 12,**

3. **ex itinere**: see chap. 6, l. 2, and note.

**oppūgnāre**: means here *carry by assault.*

5. **omnis . . . multitūdo**: notice that an adjective and a noun are often separated by words depending on the noun. Here **ex fuga** from the position is almost equivalent to **fugientium.**

6. **vīneis**: wooden frames with sloping roof and covered with hides, to protect a number of besiegers.

7. **āctis**: from **ago**, *brought up ;* the **vīneae** were often moved on wheels.

**aggere iacto**: *when earth had been thrown up for a mound.* This was done so that wooden towers could be brought up near the walls.

10. **ut cōnservārentur**: mark how often a dependent clause **precedes** the one on which it depends. Attention to this

will often help in unravelling a long sentence. Now see
**qui . . . dēdūceret**, chap. 2, l. 3 ; **quid . . . posset et
. . . audērent**, chap. 8, ll. 3, 4 ; **qui . . . morārētur**,
chap. 11, l. 6.

PAGE **29**,
line 32. **paucis dēfendentibus** : *though the defenders were few.*

PAGE **30**,

1. **Castris mūnitis** : *after making a fortified camp.* The first
   and most important thing, after selecting the site of a
   camp, was to intrench it. That may be all that is meant
   in this instance.
   **vineas agere** : depends on **coepit.**
   **quaeque . . . comparāre** : *and to get ready whatever.*
2. **ūsui** : compare **subsidio**, p. 26, l. 32.
5. **quae** : *the like of which.*

CHAP. **13**,

1. **obsidibus acceptis** : *after receiving hostages.*
   **armis . . . trāditis** : it was Cæsar's practice to disarm his
   conquered enemies.
3. **Qui cum** : the relative is in the right place in Latin, but we
   cannot translate in this order. The natural place for both
   words is at the beginning of a clause ; but when they
   come together, the relative takes precedence.
5. **circiter . . . quinque** : *only about five miles.*
6. **abesset** : governed by **cum.**
   **māiōres nātu** : *elders ;* **seniōres** would not do.
7. **sēse . . . venīre** : *they surrendered to him unconditionally.*
9. **pueri** : *children,* as **homines** often means *men and women.*

PAGE **30**,

9. **atque** : *and besides,* or *and in particular.*
17. **neque . . . contendere** : *and that they were not in arms.*
20. **passis manibus** : pitiful !

CHAP. **14**,

1. **facit verba** : *intercedes.*
2. **in fide . . . fuērunt** : *have been faithful and friendly.*
4. **perferre** : *were enduring.* For the tense, see 584 (336, A) ;
   B. 317 ; H–B. 593.

line 5. **ēius cōnsili prīncipes**: *the prime movers in this plan :* **prīn-cipes** = **auctōres**, *authors.*

6. **in Britanniam profūgērunt**: as lately Boulanger and others have done.

8. **clēmentia**: said of one who has power to exercise the opposite, **sevēritas, crūdēlitas.**

**mānsuētūdine**: said of one who is humane and gentle, opposed to **feritas.**

9. **fēceris . . . amplificābis**: we say, 'if you do this, you will add to'; in Latin, 'if you shall have done this, you will add to.'

10. **qua**: 151, e, f (105, d); B. 91, 2, 5; H. 186 (190, 1); H–B. 142.

**si qua bella**, etc.: *by whose aid and resources they* (the Ædui) *are accustomed to bear the burden of whatever wars befall them.*

PAGE **30**,

26. **perferre . . . dēfēcisse**: *were enduring . . . had revolted.*

28. **quod intellegerent**: *seeing.*

31. **sua**: emphatic; *his own*, that is, *his well-known.*

32. **quod si fēcerit**: *if he should do this;* the subjunctive of the future perfect, for which there is no separate form; hence the form of the perfect subjunctive is borrowed. If the tense is named by its form, it will be called *perfect subjunctive;* if by its meaning, *future perfect subjunctive.*

PAGE **31**,

1. **amplificātūrum (esse)**: the subject must be inferred from the subject of **fēcerit.**

CHAP. **15**,

1. **honōris . . . causa**: *out of regard to Divitiacus.*

3. **māgna . . . auctōritāte**: *one of great influence;* a predicate ablative of description; such an ablative must always have a modifier, as here, **māgna.** The genitive may be used in the same way, as below, **māgnae virtūtis.** On the order, see note, chap. 12, l. 5.

6. **quōrum**, etc.: translate closely in the order of the Latin; *about their character and customs, Cæsar, on inquiry;* so, generally, do your best to keep close to the Latin order. Read again the Introductory Note, p. 43.

line 12. **qui . . . dēdidissent**: *for having surrendered;* what would be the meaning of **qui . . . dēdiderant?**

**PAGE 31,**

    6. **hominum . . . praestābat**: *was the most populous;* what is it literally ?

    12. **patī**: *that they permitted.* Supply **eos**, referring to **Nervii**, as the subject of **patī, esse, increpitāre,** and **cōnfīrmāre.**

    13. **quod . . . exīstimārent**: observe in the simplified text **quod . . . exīstimābant**; why the difference ?

    16. **qui . . . dēdissent . . . prōiēcissent**: *for having surrendered and renounced;* literally, *since they had surrendered.*

    17. **sēse**: subject-accusative of **mīssūros.**

**CHAP. 16,**

    1. **trīduum**: *for three days,* accusative of duration.

    2. **Sabim**: now called the Sambre.

    6. **quīque**: equivalent to **et eos qui,** *and all such as.*

    **per aetātem**: *by reason of their age;* that is, whether too old or too young.

    7. **in eum locum . . . quo**: *into a place to which.* The idea of the Latin fully expressed would be, *into a place of such a character* (**eum**) *that to it* (**quo**) *there would be no access for an army.* 537, 2 (319, 2 and note) ; B. 284, 2 ; H. 591, 2 (500, I) ; H–B. 521, 1 and a. Compare **qui . . vidērentur,** immediately preceding.

    8. **exercitui**: *for an army,* not necessarily, *for Cæsar's army.*

**PAGE 31,**

    19. **Cum . . . fēcisset**: a temporal **cum** clause is not always best rendered by *when,* etc.: *after marching for three days.*

    24. **hīs . . . persuāserant**: observe on p. 29, l. 1, an example of the impersonal construction of **persuādeo** in the passive: **hīs persuādēri . . . nōn poterat,** *it was not possible for these to be persuaded.*

    27. **cōniēcisse**: the verb implies hurried action, and so differs from **dēpōno**, which Cæsar uses in Book IV., 19, of putting women and children in a place of safety.

CHAP. **17,**

line 2. **qui . . . dēligant**: compare **qui dēdūceret**, chap, 2, l. 3,
and note ; **qui . . . morārētur**, chap. 11, *l.* 6.

**Cum** : *since.* See note on chap. 6, l. 8.

5. **dēmōnstrārunt**: shortened from **dēmōnstrāvērunt**. 181,
a (128, a, 1) ; B. 116, 1 ; H. 238 (235) ; H-B. 163, 1.

**inter singulas** : *between each two;* the same mistake, "between each," is common in English.

6. **neque . . . negōti** : *and it was a matter of no difficulty
at all.*

7. **cum . . . vēnisset** : *when the first legion should reach the
camping ground.* In the direct form, **vēnerit,** *shall have
reached;* then regularly such a future perfect is changed
to the pluperfect subjunctive in indirect discourse after a
past tense. See note on chap 9, l. 10.

8. **sarcinis** : "Besides his arms, the Roman soldier carried
stakes (**vallī**), used for the palisades of the camp, food
and utensils, a saw, a spade, a chain for his prisoners,
and other things. He was loaded like a mule." —LONG.

**qua pulsa** : *if this legion were beaten.*

**futūrum (esse)** : depends on **dēmōnstrārunt** ; *the result
would be.*

9. **Nervii autem** : *now the Nervii.* **Nervii** is the subject of
**effēcerant.** This long sentence is not so difficult as it at
first seems. Follow closely the Latin order to discover
the sense, render **quo** *in order that,* **effēcerant** *had caused,*
and **instar** *like.*

11. **teneris . . . ēnātis** : *by lopping the trees when young, and
intertwining the branches which grew out thick in a lateral
direction;* **ēnātis** from **ēnāscor.**

12. **interiectis** : it does not appear possible to take this word
in the sense given to it in the dictionaries, *thrown or
stuffed in.* So Moberly translates, "by throwing in
brambles and thorns for the present occasion." But is it
to be supposed that this was done everywhere ? If not,
how would the Nervii know where to do it ? Moreover,
what they had done was done **antīquitus,** *from of old.*
Translate, therefore, *by planting among them.*

line 14. **quo nōn modo nōn . . . sed ne . . . quidem**: this for-
mula, or (without the second **nōn**) **nōn modo . . . sed
ne . . . quidem**, is usually awkwardly rendered, *not only
not, but not even*. Instead, translate as if the first member
were complete in itself (suppressing **modo**), followed by
*nay, nor even*, thus : *which it was not possible to pass through,
nay, nor even see through.*

15. **Hīs rēbus**: *by these obstacles.*

16. **nōn . . . cōnsilium**: *they ought not to disregard the advice.*

PAGE **32**,

4. **impedīmentōrum**: here, *baggage animals ;* **impedīmentis**,
below, *baggage.*

9. **Adiuvābat**: the subject is the long sentence following,
**Nervii . . . effēcerant.** Translate, *this circumstance favored
the advice of those who reported the intelligence, that* (**quod**).

10. **nihil . . . possent**: compare **quid in bello possent**, p. 24,
l. 25 ; **quid virtūte posset**, p. 27, l. 12.

11. **neque enim**: *and in fact . . . not.* Observe that **enim**
here does not mean *for.*

12. **pedestribus valent cōpiis**: compare **virtūte . . . valēre**,
p. 25, l. 5. The ablative is ablative of means.

13. **ad eos**: that is, the Nervii.

CHAP. **18**,

1. **quem locum**: *I mean the place which.*

3. **Ab eo flūmine**: that is, on the other side.

4. **pari adclīvitāte collis**: *a hill of similar upward slope;* a
descriptive ablative.

**ab superiōre parte**: *in the upper part.* **Ab** not seldom
means *on, in, at, by,* because the idea of removal (*from*)
implies previous contact or nearness, and the latent idea
is sometimes the most important.

5. **ut**: may be considered as referring to an **ita** suppressed
with **silvestris** ; *so thickly wooded that.*

**nōn . . . posset**: *one could not easily see within.* Impersonal expressions, like **perspici potest**, are common in
Latin. Mark the mode of translation.

7. **secundum**: *along,* properly *following,* from **sequor.**

PAGE 32,

line 24. **adversus huic et contrārius**: *corresponding to this and right opposite.*

25. **passus . . . apertus**: *clear of woods for about two hundred paces up from its base.*

**Infimus: ab Inferiōre parte.**

CHAP. 19,

1. **omnibus cōpiis**: Cæsar often uses **cum omnibus cōpiis.**

2. **cōnsuētūdine**: *according to custom;* just as frequently **ex cōnsuētūdine.**

4. **conlocārat**: for **conlocāverat.** See **dēmōnstrārunt,** chap. 17, l. 5, and note.

6. **praesidiōque impedīmentis**: compare **subsidio oppidānis,** chap. 7, l. 2, and note.

11. **opere dīmēnso**: *after laying out the work;* the expression refers to marking off the ground preparatory to trenching, making a rampart, etc.

**castra mūnīre**: *to make a camp.*

17. **in manibus nostris**: *close upon us.*

18. **ad**: *towards;* repeat it mentally before **eos.**

**adverso colle**: *straight up the hill;* literally, *with the hill before them;* so perhaps strictly neither an ablative absolute nor an ablative of the " way by which."

PAGE 32,

32. **ratio ōrdōque āgminis**: *the plan and the order of marching.*

**aliter . . . āc**: *otherwise than, different from what;* this strange idiom looks like an abridged, colloquial expression; probably it was, fully expressed, **aliter āc aliter,** *one way and another way.* The order of march was one way and the Belgæ had reported it another way. So I have heard a child say, " This is different and that is different," meaning " this is different from that."

PAGE 33,

8. **cum**: *while;* to be repeated mentally with **facerent.**

10. **neque . . . cēdentes Insequi audērent**: *and while our men were hesitating to pursue them when they retreated.*

**quem ad fīnem**: translate as if it were **ad fīnem ad quem,** *to the line to which the level, clear ground extended.*

line 15. **ut . . . cōnfīrmāverant**: *as they had arranged their order of battle and ranks within the woods, and as they had encouraged each other to do.*

**CHAP. 20,**

2. **sīgnum tuba dandum (erat)**: in order to call the men to take their places in the ranks. Some might not see the flag.

3. **sīgnum dandum**: this time the signal is for the charge, or perhaps to get ready for a charge.

5. **subsidio**: dative of end or service, but render as if a nominative, which might have been used, *a help.*

7. **commode**: modifies **praescrībere.**

**ipsī sibi praescrībere . . . poterant**: they could *direct themselves without any orders* (**ipsī**).

11. **nihil**: *not . . . at all;* stronger than **nōn.**

12. **per se**: *on their own responsibility.*

**quae vidēbantur**: *whatever seemed best.*

**PAGE 33,**

27. **qui**: does not refer to **mīlites,** but to **iī** understood.

**aggeris petendī causā**: *for the purpose of seeking materials for a rampart.* Mark the position of **causā,** always following the genitive depending on it.

30. **hīs difficultātibus**: *in this strait;* but the words are in the dative with **subsidio.** Find two other instances of this construction of two datives.

32. **quid fierī oportēret**: the object of **praescrībere.**

**CHAP. 21,**

1. **necessāriīs rēbus imperātīs**: when you meet with **res,** ask yourself exactly what it means, and then find a proper rendering. Translate, *after giving the necessary orders.*

4. **prīstinae**: this word is often used of what was formerly and still continues.

**neu . . . animo**: *and not lose presence of mind.*

6. **quod . . . aberant**: gives the reason of the following, not the preceding, clause.

8. **pūgnantibus occurrit**: *he finds them fighting.*

line 8. **Temporis**: mark how the important word comes first. Take this sentence in thought almost without change in the order of the words, then translate.

**tanta** . . . **exiguitas**: *so great was the littleness = such was the shortness.* Translate, *so short was the time.*

10. **Insignia**: "the crests, feathers red and black, and other decorations which the soldiers had. . . . On the march the helmet was not carried on the head. The shields had leather coverings when they were not in use." — Long.

12. **Quam** . . . **dēvēnit**: *to whatever part of the army each one happened to come.*

**ab opere**: that is, making the camp; see chap. 19, l. 11.

13. **quaeque** . . . **cōnspēxit**: *and whatever standards he caught sight of first.*

Page 34,

13. **quo** . . . **posset**: *whither a javelin could be hurled = a javelin throw.*

19. **Quam** . . . **in partem**: compare the second line of the chapter. **quisque** seems oddly placed, but it is crowded out of the first place, where it would like to stand, by **quam**.

Chap. 22,

2. **rei mīlitāris** . . . **ōrdo**: *military science and arrangement.*

3. **fiēbat**: *the result was.*

**aliae** . . . **parte**: in this idiom the second part only of the thought is expressed. ʻ *Other legions were fighting in another part* ʼ implies ʻ some were fighting in one part of the field.ʼ So **claudus altero pede**, *lame in the other foot*, implies one foot sound.

5. **interiectis**: to be taken with **saepibus**.

6. **ut**: *so that.* **conlocāri**: depends on **possent**.

7. **in**: of reason, *because of* or *owing to.*

8. **inīquitāte**: usually translated *unfavorable condition*, or by some similar phrase, and such is the common meaning of **inīquitas**; but the context shows that the meaning here is closer to the original sense, that of *unevenness*; hence we may translate, *owing to such inequality in the condition of things.*

PAGE **34**,

line 25. **cum**: *since*, governs **impedīrētur** as well as **resisterent.**

dīversīs legiōnibus : dīversus means *turned different ways, not with united line;* hence here, *disjoined.* Translate, *since, owing to the legions being separated.*

28. **neque certa subsidia** : here begins the statement of the result ; **certa subsidia** : subject of **poterant.**

**neque quid**, etc. : *nor was it possible to foresee what was needed everywhere.* After **prōvidērī** supply mentally **poterat**, of which the whole preceding clause is the grammatical subject.

CHAP. **23**,

1. **ut** : *since.* Would the mode of **cōnstiterant** have been the same, if **cum** had been used in place of **ut** ?

2. **acie** : an old form of the genitive for **aciēī.**
**Atrebates** : object of **compulērunt.**

6. **Ipsi** : refers to the subject of **interfēcērunt** ; that is, **legiōnis nōnae et decimae mīlites.**

8. **dīversae = aliae** ; what should it mean from its derivation ?

10. **a frōnte** : *along the front.* See chap. 18, l. 4, and note.

11. **ab sinistra parte** : *on the left.* Compare **ā frōnte**, preceding line, and **ab superiōre parte**, chap. 18, l. 4, and note.

**nūdātis castrīs** : *as the camp was left-unguarded.*

13. **aperto latere** : *on their* (the legions') *exposed flank.*

14. **summum . . . locum** : *the summit occupied by the camp ;* **castrōrum** is a possessive genitive.

PAGE **35**,

3. **exanimātos . . . cōnfectos** : *breathless and exhausted by wounds.*

**hīs** : the ninth and tenth legions.

4. **ea pars** : that is, **ea pars hostium.**

5. **cōnantes** : accusative, agreeing with **Atrebates** understood, or a pronoun referring to Atrebates.

8. **resistentes hostes** : object of **cōniēcērunt.**

16. **summam imperi** : *chief command.*

CHAP. **24**,

2. **cum . . . reciperent** : *as they were returning.*

5. **cum respēxissent** : *on looking back.* A **cum** clause is not always best translated by a full clause.

line 6. praecípites . . . mandābant : *ran away as fast as they could.* What literally ?

7. eōrum : depends on clāmor fremitusque.

8. ferēbantur : *began to rush.* Observe the imperfects followed by perfects. The imperfect paints, the perfect describes.

10. auxiliī causa : *for the purpose of rendering aid = as auxiliaries.*

11. cum : *since.* See note, chap. 6, l. 8.
compléri : this and the following infinitives depend on vīdissent.

13. vīdissent : the subject is equites Trēverī.

14. rēbus : *fortunes.* How might a clause be substituted here in Latin for the ablative absolute ?

15. pulsos superātōsque : supply esse.

PAGE 35,

21. pulsos : supply esse.

22. adversīs hostibus occurrēbant : *came straight against the enemy.* What literally ?

23. cālōnes . . . āc summo iugo : the porta decumāna was the rear gate of the camp, opposite the porta praetōria. It appears from this passage that the place for the cālōnes was at the back of the camp, and that in this instance the camp was partly on sloping ground.

30. virtūtis opīnio : *reputation for valor.*

PAGE 36,

2. dīversos dissipātōsque : *running in different directions and scattered.*

5. hostes : subject-accusative of potītos (esse).

CHAP. 25,

2. suos urgērī : *that his men were hard pressed;* the infinitive depends on vīdit.

3. cōnfertos mīlites : *that the soldiers by being crowded together.*
sibi . . . impedīmento : *hindered one another.*

8. ut . . . posset : *so that he could no longer stand.*

9. Hīs rēbus : *for these reasons.*
tardiōres : *were losing heart.*

12. subeuntes intermittere : *cease mounting the hill.*

line 12. **ab utrōque latere** : *on both flanks.* Compare **ab superiōre parte**, chap. 18, l. 4.

13. **rem . . . angusto** : *that the situation was critical.* What literally ?

14. **ūni** : a peculiar use of **ūnus**, quite equivalent to *a;* not to be imitated in writing Latin.

17. **sīgna . . . iūssit** : *he ordered them to advance and at the same time to open out their ranks.*

PAGE **36,**

7. **Caesar** : subject of **prōcessit**, fifteen lines below. This first sentence extending through eighteen lines looks very formidable ; but if it is taken in accordance with the Introductory Note, p. 43, the meaning will be evident. To translate the sentence is more difficult. In translating, repeat "*and saw*" before the words **quartae cohortis,** and render the ablative absolutes by clauses, thus : *and saw that all the captains of the fourth cohort were killed.* Then, **reliquos esse tardiōres,** *that the rest* (in consequence) *were losing heart.*

8. **sīgnīsque . . . conlātīs** : *and since the standards were brought together.* Try constantly to make out the relation in thought expressed by participles ; that is, whether the idea is that of time, *when, while*, etc. ; of cause, *as, since ;* of concession, *though, notwithstanding ;* or of condition, accompanying circumstances, etc., to be variously rendered.

16. **ab novissimis** : *in the rear.* So below, l. 21. Compare **ab sinistra parte**, p. 23, l. 13. In both places in this chapter it would be easy to make the mistake of taking **ab** in the sense of **ex**, as a substitute for the partitive genitive.

27. **operam nāvāre cuperet** : "*wished to do his best.*" What literally ?

CHAP. **26,**

3. **ut . . . coniungerent** : *for the legions gradually to draw together.*

7. **proelio nūntiāto** : *on the report of the battle.*
**cursu incitāto** : *quickening their speed.* The participle following is causal ; they began to run because of the report of the battle.

line 10. **qui**: refers to **decimam legiōnem**. What is the grammatical irregularity, and how is it to be accounted for? **cum**: to be taken with **cōgnōvissent**.

**quo in loco res esset** : *what the situation was.* What literally ? Account for the subjunctive.

12. **nihil . . . fēcērunt**: *left nothing undone in the way of speed.* What literally ?

**reliqui**: neuter of **reliquus.** A partitive genitive depending on **nihil.** Find a similar construction in chap. 15.

PAGE 36,

31. **conversa signa** : the object of **Inferrent**, but most conveniently rendered as coördinate with it, *to face about and charge.* It is thought that by this movement the twelfth and the seventh legions formed a circle or a square.

PAGE 37,

1. **neque timērent**: repeat **cum** mentally from the preceding clause ; *and since they* (no longer) *feared.*

**āversi** : literally, *being turned away;* translate, *from their rear being unguarded.*

CHAP. 27,

2. **vulneribus cōnfecti** : *badly wounded.* What literally ? **prōcubuissent** : from **prōcumbo.**

3. **vēro** : emphasizes **equites**, but is better left untranslated ; say, *while the cavalry.*

4. **se . . . praeferrent**: *thrust themselves before ;* a result clause, dependent on **tanta . . . est facta.**

5. **in extrēma spe salūtis** : "*when all hope of saving themselves was at an end.*" Here a literal translation would be meaningless or misleading.

7. **proximi . . . Insistēbant**: *those nearest would stand upon their prostrate companions.*

8. **his dēiectis** : *when these* (in turn) *were thrown down.*

10. **intercepta remittēbant** : *would catch and hurl back.* See **ēductas Instrūxerant**, chap. 8, l. 17, and note.

11. **ut**, etc. : *so that one ought to judge that it was not without cause that men of such valor.* On **iūdicāre dēbēret**, compare **perspici posset**, chap. 18, l. 5, and note.

line 13. **quae . . . difficillimis**: *things which, most difficult in themselves.*

**facilia**: a predicate adjective with **redēgerat**.

PAGE 37,

15. **innĪxi**: from **innĪtor**, agrees with **nostri**.

**perterritos**: supply **esse**; the subject-accusative is **hostes**.

16. **inermes**: agrees with **cālōnes**, *even though unarmed.*

23. **qui superessent**: *the survivors.* Supply **ii** as antecedent of **qui**.

**ut**: *as.* So used p. 34, l. 23.

24. **cōnicerent**: dependent on **tantam virtutem . . . ut**; (so that) *those who survived* (**qui superessent**) *kept hurling.*

CHAP. 28,

1. **prope**: modifies **ad**, not **redācto**.

2. **redācto**: see the last word of the preceding chapter.

**māiōres nātu**: see chap. 13, l. 6, and note.

3. **pueris**: see chap. 13, l. 9, and note.

4. **cōnsēnsu . . . supererant**: *with the consent of all the survivors.*

7. **vix ad**: *to barely;* for **ad vix**, as some say.

8. **in**: *towards;* **erga** might have been used.

9. **vidērētur**: not *that he might seem,* but *that he might be seen.*

11. **se . . . prohibērent**: *refrain and keep their dependents from;* **prohibēre** is appropriate to **suos**, but hardly to **se**.

PAGE 37,

31. **aestuāria**: "the country lying to the north (the modern Zealand) is low and marshy, cut up with tidewater inlets and bays." — ALLEN & GREENOUGH.

32. **cum vīctōribus**, etc.: *since they thought there was no obstacle for the victors, no safety for the vanquished.*

PAGE 38,

4. **mīlibus LX.**: they had promised fifty thousand; see chap. 4. It was natural that they should exaggerate their losses.

CHAP. 29,

1. **auxilio Nerviis**: compare **subsidio oppidānis**, chap. 7, l. 2, and note. Find other examples of this construction.

4. **ūnum oppidum**: supposed to be at the junction of the Sambre and Meuse.

5. **ex omnibus in circuitu partibus**: simply, *all round.*

line 9. **conlocābant**: there is a reading, **conlocārant**. If that is the true reading, **tum** in the preceding line would mean *besides*.

10. **cum**: *while*. Four lines below **cum** means *though*.

16. **aditus . . . pedum**: *an approach of two hundred feet in breadth, not more;* **pedum** depends on **aditus**.

21. **iis impedīmentis**: take with **dēpositis**, two lines below.

22. **agere āc portāre**: *drive or carry*.

24. **ūna**: *with it;* that is, the plunder.

25. **cum alias**, etc.: *since they carried on now aggressive now defensive war*. What literally?

1. **prīmo adventu** = **cum prīmum advēnisset**, *as soon as our army had got there*.

3. **pedum** xii.: that is, **in altitūdinem**, which is expressed, chap. 5, 1. 19.

4. **oppido**: might have been **in oppido**. Cf. **castris**, chap. 11, l. 5.

5. **vīneis āctis**: **āctis** from **ago**; see chap. 12, l. 6, and note.
**aggere exstrūcto**: an embankment of timber, stones, and earth was begun at a distance from the walls of a town, wide enough to roll one or more towers upon, and was carried forward by soldiers working under the shelter of the **vīneae** up to the defensive works.

6. **cōnstitui**: *being raised*.

7. **ab tanto spatio**: *so far away*. Compare **ab mīlibus**, chap. 7, l. 6, and note.

8. **quibusnam manibus**: *with what hands, pray;* **nam** added for emphasis, to point their sarcasm.

10. **conlocāre**: strangely used for **conlocātūros (esse)**. The Aduatuci may have thought that the Romans intended to hoist the tower upon their wall, or they may have been joking. Which is more likely?

5. **hominibus . . . contemptui**: another pair of datives. Find other examples. The Italians of the present time do not strike one as conspicuously shorter than the Germans.

line 5. **mǎgnitūdine**: being contrasted with **brevitas**, is used in the sense of **altitūdine**.

Chap. 31,

1. **movēri**: *moving*. This word here has suggested a change of **conlocāre**, in the last line of the preceding chapter, to **mōtūros**, a very plausible conjecture, but it spoils the joke of the Aduatuci.

5. **qui**: *since they*. Compare **qui . . . dēdidissent**, chap. 15, l. 12, and note.

8. **pro sua clēmentia**: *according to his well-known clemency*. See chap. 14, l. 8, and note. What did they think of his clemency when he sold 53,000 of them into slavery?

11. **trāditis armis = si arma trādidissent**, *if they should surrender their arms*.

13. **per cruciātum interfici**: *to be tortured to death*. What literally?

Page 39,

16. **statuisset**: not *had decided*, but *should decide*. No mistake is oftener made by beginners than in the rendering of a pluperfect subjunctive of indirect discourse representing a future perfect of direct discourse. Such a subjunctive is to be rendered by the auxiliary *should*, not *had*. To tell whether a pluperfect subjunctive represents a future perfect, think what form a speaker's words would take, remembering that the Romans commonly used the future or future perfect of things really future, while we very often use the present.

Chap. 32,

1. **cōnsuētūdine**: ablative of cause.

3. **aries**: "a long, strong beam of wood, furnished with an iron head in the form of a ram's head. It was suspended from a framework by a strong chain or ropes, and worked by men, who drove it against the wall." — Long.

4. **in Nerviis**: *in the case of the Nervii;* a common meaning of **in** with names of persons.

5. **ne quam . . . inferant**: *not to do any harm to those who had surrendered to the Roman people.*

line 7 **facere**: one would expect the future with subject-accusative, **se factūros** (**esse**). Compare **conlocāre**, for conlocātūros **esse**, chap. 30, l. 10.

9. **prope . . . adaequārent**: *came up almost to the very top;*
**summam** with **altitūdinem**. What literally ?

12. **pāce sunt ūsi** = **conquiēvērunt**, *kept quiet.*

CHAP. **33,**

3. **nostros**: *our commanders*, subject-accusative of **dēductū-**
**ros** and **servātūros** (**esse**).

**praesidia**: men stationed in the **castella** ; see below.

4. **dēductūros . . . servātūros**: observe how frequently
**esse** is omitted with the future participle.

**dēnique**: *at any rate.* What is its usual meaning?

5. **tertia vigilia**: the Romans divided the night into four
equal divisions, watches, of about three hours each.

9. **eo concursum est**: *the soldiers hurried thither.* What literally ? Find similar constructions in chaps. 6, 9, 10, 11.

10. **in extrēma spe salūtis**: compare chap. 27, l. 5, and note.
The context shows, however, that the meaning is not
quite the same here. Translate, *as their last chance of
saving themselves.*

14. **nēmo**: observe the emphasis from its position. Compare
in English, "Silver and gold have I none." **nēmo** and
**nūllus** are often so placed. Cf. **nūlli**, chap. 6, l. 10.

16. **ab iis qui ēmerant** = **ab ēmptōribus**: *by the purchasers*,
who were the **mercātōres**, traders who followed the
army as hungry sharks follow a ship.

**capitum**: we say "souls." It depends on **quīnquāginta**
**trium**.

17. **quīnquāginta trium**: 53,000 captives, probably chained
in gangs and sent to be sold in the Province and in
Italy ; a source of great gain to the general.

PAGE **40,**

4. **mīlites . . . mīlitibus**: another evidence of haste. See
p. 26, l. 19, and note.

5. **ne quam . . . iniūriam**: see p. 39, l. 28, and note.

9. **iis**: with **armis**. Observe the order of the words.

line 10. **vīminibus intextis**: repeat mentally **ex** before these words. Some supply **factis**.

16. **pūgnātumque**, etc.: translate as if **hostibus** and **viris** were subjects.

17. **ut ... dēbuit**: *as brave men ought to fight.* What literally ?

18. **iacerent**: the subjunctive shows that the remark is a general one. The indicative would have a limiting force The difference can hardly be brought out in translation. In the former case we may render, *against men who could throw;* in the latter, *against those who were throwing.*

20. **ad = circiter.**

CHAP. **34,**

2. **miserat**: *had sent*, that is, before the defeat of the Aduatuci.

5. **dicīōnem**: *under the sway;* in some texts, **in dēditiōnem**. If that reading is correct, the meaning would be, *were brought to surrender.*

CHAP. **35,**

1. **pācāta**: see p. 23, l. 7, and note.

4. **qui ... pollicērentur**: compare p. 23, l. 19, **qui ... dēdūceret**; p. 29, l. 12, **qui ... morārētur**; p. 31, l. 30, **qui ... dēligant.**

6. **inita proxima aestāte**: see p. 23, l. 18, and note.

10. **ex litteris**: *in consequence of the letters.*

11. **supplicātio**: a public, religious festival of thanksgiving, decreed by the senate. "The fifteen days' rejoicing marks the constant fear of the Gauls which had haunted the Romans ever since the 'dies Alliensis.' Kraner remarks that the longest 'supplicatio' till this had been one of twelve days, for Pompeius' success against Mithridates." — MOBERLY.

**nūlli**: see p. 40, l. 22; also p, 26, l. 24, and note.

# EXERCISES ON SIMPLIFIED TEXT.

—◦◦—

The references are to the Grammars of Allen and Greenough, Bennett (B.),
Harkness (H.), and Hale and Buck (H-B.). References in parentheses are to the
old editions.

The learner is expected, before writing the Exercises, to review the Latin text,
and find therein and commit to memory illustrations of the grammatical principles
selected.

## CHAPTER I.

1. Indirect Discourse : 579, 580 (336, 1 and 2) ; B. 313, 314; H.
642 (523 and I) ; H-B. 534, 1, 2, 589.

2. **Cum** Temporal with Subjunctive : 545, 548 (325) ; B. 288, B ;
H. 600, II (521, II and 2) ; H-B, 524.

3. Subjunctive after Verbs of Fearing : 564 (331, f) ; B. 296, 2 ;
H. 567, 1 (498, III) ; H-B. 502, 4.

1. Cæsar was in hither Gaul.

2. Reports were brought into hither Gaul.

3. While Labienus was in Gaul, the Belgæ made a league.[1]

4. A report is brought that [2] the Belgæ are conspiring.

5. They are afraid that our army is coming [3] against them.

6. They are vexed [4] that our army remains in Gaul.

7. Cæsar feared that the Belgæ were conspiring.

8. Letters kept coming,[5] while they were conspiring.

NOTES. — [1] made a league : one word in Latin. [2] Be careful about
the *that*-clause in this and the following sentence. Recall the text to
memory and mentally apply the rules. [3] is coming : use **venio**. [4] are
vexed : in Latin one of the expressions, like **rūmōrēs adferēbantur**,
requiring the accusative and infinitive. [5] kept coming : one word in
Latin.

## CHAPTER II.

1. Relative Clauses of Purpose : 531, 2 and ɴ. (317, 2 and ɴ.) ;
B. 282, 2 and a; H. 590 (497, I) ; H–B. 502, 2.

2. Accus. and Infin. of Indirect Discourse : 579, 580 (336, 1 and 2) ;
B. 313, 314 ; H. 642 (523 and I) ; H–B. 534, 1, 2, 589.

. 1.ˈ In hither Gaul there[1] were two legions.

2. Two new legions Cæsar levies.

3. The two new legions are sent into the interior of Gaul.

4. Cæsar sends his lieutenant to lead[2] them.[3]

5. Pedius was sent to lead the new legions.

6. The Senones report that the Belgians are gathering.[4]

7. The Senones informed Cæsar about the Belgians.

NOTES. —[1] there : omit. [2] to lead : do not express a purpose in
Latin by the infinitive. [3] them : **eas**. [4] are gathering : a passive
form in Latin, because the sense is, *are being collected together.*

## CHAPTER III.

1. Ablative of Means : 409 (248, 8, c) ; B. 218 ; H. 476 (420) ; H–B.
423.

2. Ablative with **potior**, ūtor, etc. : 410 (249) ; B. 218, 1 ; H. 477
(421, I) ; H–B. 429.

3. Accus. and Infin. of Indirect Discourse : 580 (336, 2) ; B. 314 ;
H. 642 (523, I) ; H–B. 534, 1, 2.

1. ˈCæsar came unexpectedly to the borders of the Remi.

2. The Remi said they had not combined[1] against the
Roman people.

3. They said they were ready to give hostages.

4. All the rest of the Belgæ[2] had joined[3] with the
Germans.

5. They aided Cæsar with corn and other[4] things.

6. The Remi and their[5] kinsmen enjoy the same laws.

Notes. — [1] they had not combined : *themselves not to have combined.*
[2] of the Belgæ : not the genitive. [3] had joined : in Latin, *had joined themselves,* if you use **coniungo.** [4] **aliis.** [5] their : omit.

## Chapter IV.

1. Indirect Questions : 574, 575 (334) ; B. 300 ; H. 649, II (529, 1) ; H–B. 537, 507, 3.

2. Substantive Clauses of Result : 568 (832) ; B. 297 ; H. 571, 1 (501) ; H–B. 521, 3, a.

1. Whence[1] did very many of the Belgæ[2] spring ?

2. Cæsar asked whence very many of the Belgæ sprung.

3. What states are in arms ?

4. Cæsar asked what states were in arms.

5. While Divitiacus was king, he was most powerful.

6. From Galba's foresight and justice it results that he is a powerful king.

7. From the valor of the Bellovaci it came about that they demanded the management[3] of the war.

Notes. — [1] Whence : **unde.** [2] of the Belgæ : not the genitive.
[3] management : **summa.**

## Chapter V.

1. Interest with Gen. of Person : 355 (222) ; B. 210, 211 ; H. 449, 1 (406, III) ; H–B. 345.

2. Infin. with Subject-Accus. as Subject : 452 (270) ; B. 330 ; H. 615 (538) ; H–B. 585, 597.

3. Infin. with Subject-Accus. as Object : 459, 561, a (272 and Rem.) ; B. 331 ; H. 414 (534) ; H–B. 589.

1. The children of the leading men are brought to Cæsar as hostages.

2. He orders all the children to be brought to him.[1]

3. It concerns Cæsar for [2] the senate to come to him.

4. It concerns Divitiacus to send the forces of the Ædui.

5. Cæsar sees that [3] the forces of the Belgæ are hastening.

6. He learns that the Axona is not far away.

7. This river he crossed [4] and protected his camp by means of its banks.

NOTES. — [1] him: in Latin, *himself.*  [2] for: not to be expressed in Latin.  [3] that: be careful about *that*-clauses.  [4] he crossed: use **trānseo.**

## CHAPTER VI.

1. Ablative of Separation: 400 (243); B. 214; H. 461, 462 (413); H–B. 408.

2. **Cum** Causal with Subjunctive: 549 (326); B. 286, 2; H. 598 (517); H–B. 526.

3. Ablative Absolute: 419, 420 (255 and note on p. 262); B. 227 and a; H. 489 (431); H–B. 421.

1. The enemy formed a testudo and advanced close to [1] the wall.

2. The enemy having hurled stones [2] made a testudo.

3. Since there were so many,[3] they undermined the wall.

4. They easily cleared the walls of soldiers.

5. The Belgæ having cleared the wall made an attack.[4]

6. Having made an attack [5] they threw missiles against the wall.

7. Since the missiles were many, no one was able to stand on the wall.

NOTES. — [1] advanced close to: one word in Latin.  [2] having hurled stones: say, *stones having been hurled.*  Why?  [3] so many: **tot.**  [4] attack: use **impetus.**  [5] Having made an attack: not **impetum facti.**

## Chapter VII.

1. Ablative of Cause: 404 (245); B. 219; H. 475 (416); H-B. 444.

2. Perfect Participles of Deponents: 190, b (135, b); B. 356, 2; H. 222, 1 (231, 1); H-B. 291, d.

1. At midnight archers and slingers were sent by Cæsar to the town.

2. On account of the assistance of the archers and slingers, the people in the town [1] had good hopes.

3. The enemy had no hope of taking [2] the town, because of the coming of Cæsar's soldiers.

4. Cæsar, delaying [3] a little while, sent aid to Iccius.

5. The enemy, after laying waste the fields, hastened against Cæsar's camp.

NOTES. — [1] people in the town: one word in Latin.   [2] of taking: **expúgnandi**.   [3] delaying: not present participle.

## Chapter VIII.

1. Indirect Questions: 574, 575 (334); B. 300; H. 649, II (529, I); H-B. 507, 3, 537.

2. Partitive Genitive: 346 (216); B. 201; H. 440, 5 (396, IV); H-B. 346.

1. What can the enemy do by their valor?

2. Cæsar tries what the valor of the enemy is capable of. [1]

3. How much do our men dare?

4. Cæsar makes trial of the daring [2] of his men.

5. How much space can Cæsar's army occupy?

6. Cæsar explains [3] over how much space the hill extended in front.

NOTES. — [1] is capable of: *can*.   [2] the daring of, etc.: recast the sentence mentally before translating, thus: *Cæsar makes trial what his men dare*.   [3] explains: **docet**.

## CHAPTER IX.

1. Clauses of Purpose: 530, 531 (317 and 1); B. 282; H. 568 (497, II); H–B. 502, 2.
2. The Gerundive: 158, d, 2 and 503 (113, d, 2 and 296); B. 339; H. 625–631 (544, 1); H–B. 610, 612.

1. He begins to[1] cross the river.
2. They began to lead their forces across.
3. They lead their forces over in order to take the redoubt.
4. Cæsar has shown that the river was behind him.[2]
5. They will cross so as to lay waste the lands of the Remi.

NOTES. —[1] He begins to: *makes a beginning of.*   [2] him: should it be **eum** or **se** ?

## CHAPTER X.

1. Passive of Intransitive Verbs: 372 (230); B. 256, 3, 187, 2, b; H. 302, 6 (301, 1); H–B. 364, 2, 292, a.
2. Accusative of Limit: 427, 2, 428, k (258, b and N. 1); B. 182; H. 419, 1 (380, II, 2); H–B. 385, b, 450, b, 454.
3. Substantive Clauses of Purpose: 563 (331 and N. 1); B. 295, 296; H. 564, I, 565–567 (498); H–B. 502, 3, a, 587, b.

1. Those of the Belgæ who were not killed returned home.
2. They resolve to fight in their own territories.
3. They decide that it is best[1] to lead over their army.
4. Divitiacus cannot be persuaded[2] to advance to an unfavorable place.
'5. The Ædui were persuaded to return to their homes.
6. The enemy advancing into the river were surrounded.

NOTES. —[1] that it is best: *it to be best.*   [2] recast the clause before trying to turn it into Latin.

## Chapter XI.

1. Ablative of Time: 423 (256); B. 230, 231; H. 486 (429); H-B. 439.

2. Perfect Participles: 493, 1 and 2 (290, d, 1 and 2); B. 356, 2; H. 640, 4 (550, N. 4); H-B. 602, 1 and a.

1. On the departure of the enemy Cæsar sent ahead all his cavalry.

2. At sunset the three legions returned[1] into camp.

3. In the second watch they attacked the enemy's rear.

4. The Belgæ, fearing[2] an attack, set out at daybreak.

5. The spies, having seen[3] the fugitives, bring back word.[4]

6. Cæsar, after keeping his soldiers in camp, ordered Labienus to set out.

NOTES. —[1] returned: two words in Latin.   [2] fearing: the participle **veritus** does not usually denote time *prior* to that of the main verb in the sentence, like most perfect participles, but the same time.   [3] having seen: do not say **vīsī**.   [4] bring back word: use **renûntio.**

## Chapter XII.

1. Ablative of Cause; 404 (245); B. 219; H. 475 (413); H-B. 444.

2. Ablative Absolute: 419 and 420, N. (255 and note on p. 262); B. 227 and a; H. 489 (431); H-B. 421.

1. Cæsar could not take the town on account of the great number[1] of the Suessiones.

2. Owing to[2] the works of the Romans, their "vineæ" and towers, the Suessiones send envoys.[3]

3. The next day Cæsar made a forced march and[4] tried to take the town.

4. The townsmen,[5] making a surrender, got their request.[6]

5. Because of their surrender they got their request.

6. The surrender made, they were spared.

NOTES. —[1] great number: one word in Latin. [2] Owing to: like " on account of," not separately expressed in Latin. [3] envoys: use **lēgātus**. [4] made a forced march and: a different turn in Latin. [5] townsmen : use **oppidānus**. [6] got their request: one word.

## CHAPTER XIII.

1. **Cum** Temporal with Subjunctive : 546 (325) ; B. 288, b ; H. 600, II (521, II, 2) ; H–B. 524.

2. Constructions with **peto**: 396, a (239, c, N. 1); H. 411, 4 (374, 2, N. 4) ; H–B. 393, c.

1. When the arms had been given up,[1] the elders came forth.

2. All the elders came out at Bratuspantium and begged Cæsar for peace.[2]

3. Cæsar, when he had received their submission, asked the men for their [3] arms.

4. According to their [4] custom they stretched out their hands and asked the Romans for peace.

NOTES. — [1] Render this clause in two ways : first by two words, then by a full clause. So each of the three following sentences contains a clause to be rendered in two ways. [2] Cæsar for peace: quite otherwise in Latin. [3] their: omit. [4] their: is this to be expressed by **eōrum** ?

## CHAPTER XIV.

1. Ablative of Means : 409 (248, 8, c) ; B. 218 ; H. 476 (420) ; H–B. 423.

2. Ablative with **ūtor**, etc. : 410 (249) ; B. 218, 1 ; H. 477 (421, I) ; H–B. 429.

1. Divitiacus intercedes for the conquered Belgæ.

2. Divitiacus begs that Cæsar will show [1] clemency.

3. Cæsar will exercise kindness toward the Belgæ.

4. By the help of the Belgæ the Ædui sustain wars.

5. Divitiacus says the chiefs had fled to [2] Britain.

6. If you show [3] clemency, you will increase our influence.

7. Whatever [4] war befalls, by means of their [5] resources we shall be able to hold out.

NOTES. — [1] will show: not the future in Latin. [2] to: not **ad.** [3] show : not well rendered by present indicative. [4] whatever : *if any.* [5] their : **eōrum.**

## CHAPTER XV.

1. Partitive Genitive: 346 (216) ; B. 201 ; H. 440, 5 (396, IV) ; H-B. 346.

2. Ablative of Quality: 415 (251) ; B. 224 ; H. 473, 2 (419, II) ; H-B. 443.

3. Causal Relative Sentences: 535, e (320, e) ; B. 283, 3 ; H. 592 (517) ; H-B. 523.

1. The territories of the Nervii border on the Ambiani.

2. The Nervii blame the Ambiani for having surrendered.[1]

3. The Nervii have [2] great influence among the Belgæ.

4. They use no wine, because it weakens [3] character.

5. Those men think minds lose energy through wine.

NOTES. — [1] for having surrendered : turn by a relative clause. [2] have : say *are* (men) *of.* [3] because it weakens : a relative clause with subjunctive, to indicate their view, as distinguished from a statement of fact.

## CHAPTER XVI.

1. Comparative **amplius**, etc. : 407, c (247, c) ; B. 217, 3 ; H. 471, 4 (417, N. 2) ; H-B. 416, d.

2. Accusative of Time and Space : 423 and 425 (256 and 257) ; B. 181 ; H. 417 (379) ; H-B. 387, I, II.

1. The Nervii were distant a three days' march.

2. Cæsar finds out that they are ten miles distant.

3. He learns from prisoners what the Nervii are doing.[1]

4. They have taken a position more than five miles from the Sambre.

5. He learns from prisoners that he [2] is waited for by the Nervii.

NOTES. — [1] are doing: be careful about the mode.  [2] that he : *himself.*

## CHAPTER XVII.

1. Use of **quisquam** : 312 (202, c) ; B. 252, 4 ; H. 513 (457) ; H-B. 276, 7.

2. Relative Clauses of Purpose : 530 (317) ; B. 282, 2 and **a** ; H. 590 (497, I) ; H-B. 502, 2.

3. Substitutes for Partitive Gen. : 346, c (216, c) ; B. 201, 1, **a** ; H. 444 (397, N. 3) ; H-B. 346, e.

1. Certain of the Belgæ went by night to the camp of the Nervii.

2. Cæsar says that certain men went [1] to the Nervii.

3. Many of the prisoners found out about the legions.

4. They were sent to their friends to report [2] the matter.

5. To lop trees is a matter [3] of no difficulty at all.

6. Men were sent ahead to select [4] a suitable place.

NOTES. — [1] went: *to have gone.*  [2] to report: not the infinitive. [3] matter, etc. : recast before trying to turn into Latin.  [4] to select : try two ways.

## CHAPTER XVIII.

1. Descriptive Ablative : 415 (251) ; B. 224 ; H. 473, II (419, II) ; H-B. 443.

2. Clauses of Result : 536, 537 (319) ; B. 284 ; H. 570, 591, 2 (500, I and II) ; H-B. 521, 1, e.

1. Along the river Sambre were trees [1] of great height.[2]

2. Among these trees the Nervii keep themselves hidden.

3. So [3] close together [4] were these trees that the Romans could not see through.

4. The river is of such depth that men can cross.

5. On the open ground are pickets of great courage.

NOTES. — [1] trees: **arbor**, fem.   [2] height: the same word that means *depth*.   [3] So: **ita**.   [4] close together: **crēber**.

## CHAPTER XIX.

1. Dative of Service: 382, 1, N. 1 (233 a); B. 191; H. 433 (390); H-B. 360 and a, b.

2. Imperfect of Repeated Action: 470 (277); B. 260, 2; H. 534, 3 (469, II); H-B. 484.

3. Ablative of Manner: 412 and b (248 and Rem.); B. 220; H. 473, 3 (419, III); H-B. 445 and 1.

1. The cavalry of the enemy kept making attacks.

2. They would attack our horsemen with great courage.

3. These horsemen had been sent ahead by Cæsar as a protection to the camp.

4. Again and again did the enemy pour forward from the woods, where they had hidden.

5. The slingers and archers helped [1] the horsemen.

6. With great speed they would run as far as [2] the woods.

7. With wonderful bravery they engage in battle with the Nervii.

NOTES. — [1] helped: two words in Latin.   [2] as far as: **ad**, or **usque ad**.

## CHAPTER XX.

1. The Gerundive: 158, d, 1(113, d); B. 337, 8; H. 237 (234); H-B. 609.

2. Dative of Apparent Agent: 374 (232); B. 189; H. 431 (388); H-B. 373, 1.

3. Ablative of Agent with **ā** or **ab**: 405 (246); B. 216; H. 468 (415, I); H-B. 406, 1.

1. The soldiers are directed [1] by Cæsar.
2. The soldiers must be directed by Cæsar.
3. The flag was displayed by the soldiers.
4. The flag had to be displayed by the soldiers.
5. Experience is often helpful [2] to soldiers.
6. The work is hindered by [3] the near approach [4] of the enemy.

NOTES. — [1] are directed : use **doceo**.   [2] helpful : turn by a noun.
[3] by the near approach : why not **ā** or **ab** ?   [4] near approach : one word.

### CHAPTER XXI.

1. Ablative of Gerundive with Prepositions: 507 (301); cf. B. 338, 4, b; H. 629 (544, 2); H-B. 612, IV.
2. Gerundive Construction instead of Gerund : 503 (296); B. 339; H. 625–631 (544, 1); H-B. 610, 613.
3. Purpose expressed by Gerundive : 533 and b (318 and b); B. 337, 8, b, 2 ; H. 622 (544, 2, N. 2); H-B. 612, III.

1. In looking for his shield a soldier lost time.
2. Time is wanting for putting on a helmet.
3. Seeing [1] the standards, each one went forward.
4. A line was drawn up [2] to resist [3] the enemy's charge.
5. Cæsar encouraged the tenth legion for the purpose of strengthening [4] their courage.

NOTES. — [1] Seeing: not the gerundive.   [2] A line was drawn up: see chap. xx.   [3] resist : **sustineo**.   [4] strengthening : use **cōnfīrmo**.

### CHAPTER XXII

Clauses of Result with ut (ut nōn) : 536, 537 (319) ; B. 284 ; H. 570 (500, II); H-B. 521, 1, e.

1. So dense was the hedge that it obstructed the view.
2. The result was that no legion could execute orders.

3. One legion opposes the foe in one part, another in another.

## CHAPTER XXIII.

1. Place to which: 426, 2 (258); B. 182; H. 418 (380, I); H-B. 385, b, 450, b, 454.

2. Place from which: 426, 1 (258); B. 229; H. 461 (412, I); H-B. 408.

3. Place in which: 426, 3 and 429, b (258, 4, and 260, b); B. 228; H. 483, 485 (425, 1); H-B. 433, 406, 2.

1. The Roman soldiers drive the enemy, exhausted by wounds, into an unfavorable place.

2. They followed them up from the left part of the line.

3. As they attempted[1] to cross the river, a great part of them were put to the sword.

4. In another part many of the Belgians were killed.

5. On the front the Belgæ pushed for the camp.

6. But at last they were put to flight.

NOTE. — [1] attempted: recast the sentence and express *as they attempted* by a participle referring to *a great part.*

## CHAPTER XXIV.

1. Position of **causa** with genitive: 404, c (245, c); B. 198, 1; II-B. 339, d.

2. Temporal Clauses with **cum**: 545, 546 (325); B. 288, b; H. 600, II (521, II, 2); H-B. 524, 550, a, N. 1.

1. The Romans see that the horsemen are scared.

2. Horsemen were coming to Cæsar to render aid.

3. When the camp-followers had gone out for the purpose of plundering, they saw that our men were fleeing.

4. Seeing the slingers flee,[1] they fled themselves.[2]

NOTES. — [1] flee, *to flee.*   [2] themselves: use **ipse.**

## CHAPTER XXV.

1. Ablative Absolute: 419 and a (255 and a); B. 227 and a; H. 489 (431, 4); H–B. 421.
2. Perfect Participles of Deponents: 492 (290, d); B. 356, 2; H. 192, 2 (195, 2); H–B. 602, 1, a.
3. Substitutes for Perf. Act. Partc.: 493, 2 (290, d, 2); B. 356, 2; H. 640, 4 (550, N. 4); H–B. 602, 1.

1. Cæsar saw that the soldiers of the twelfth legion were hard pushed.

2. Cæsar, seeing[1] the soldiers of the twelfth legion hard pushed, went to the right wing.

3. As[2] all the standard-bearers were wounded, the standards were lost.

4. Then Cæsar snatched a shield from a soldier.

5. The soldiers renewed their courage and delayed[3] the enemy's attack.

NOTES. — [1] seeing: not well rendered **videns**; try casting into a clause— first with **ubi**, then with **cum**.   [2] As . . . wounded: use a participial construction.   [3] renewed and delayed: it is better not to turn into Latin by coördinate verbs.

## CHAPTER XXVI.

1. Partitive•Genitive: 346 (216); B. 201; H. 441–444 (397); H–B. 346.
2. Indirect Questions: 574, 575 (334); B. 300; H. 649, II, 652 (529, I and II); H–B. 507, 3, 537.
3. Dative of Service and of Object: 382 and 1 (233 and a); B. 191; H. 433 (390); H–B. 360 and a, b.

1. One was sent for assistance to another.[1]

2. The soldiers of two legions guarded the baggage.[2]

3. He saw in how great peril the camp was.

4. They will leave nothing undone [3] in point of courage.

5. He will report to me in what state the army is.

6. He saw that the tenth was fighting very bravely.

NOTES. — [1] another: bring the two forms of **alius** together. [2] guarded the baggage: make a different turn. [3] leave nothing undone: a strange Latin idiom.

## CHAPTER XXVII.

1. Temporal Clauses with **cum**: 545, 546 (325); B. 288, b; H. 600, II (521, 2); H–B. 524, 550, a, N. 1.

2. Clauses of Result with **ut (ut nōn)**: 536, 537 (319); B. 284; H. 570 (500, II); H–B. 521, 1, e.

3. Clauses of Purpose with **ut (nē, ut nē)**: 530, 531 (317); B. 282; H. 568 (497, II); H–B. 502, 2.

1. So great is the courage of the Nervii that they fight from the heaps of corpses.

2. Ascending [1] very high banks, they displayed the greatest courage.

3. They dared to cross a wide stream in order to renew the fight.

4. The cavalry, to wipe out [2] their disgrace, advance even into a disadvantageous position.

5. The greatness of their spirit rendered difficult things easy.

NOTES. — [1] Ascending: turn by a clause with **cum**. [2] to wipe out: not the infinitive.

## CHAPTER XXVIII.

1. Ablative of Separation: 400 (243); B. 214; H. 461 (413); H–B. 408.

2. Substitutes for Partitive Genitive: 346, c (216, c); B. 201, 1, a; H. 444 (397, N. 3); H–B. 346, e.

3. Substantive Clauses of Purpose with **ut (nē)** : 563 (331) ; B. 295, 296 ; H. 565 (498); H–B. 502, 3, **a.**

1. Of five hundred senators, three were left.

2. Out of forty (**quadrāgintā**) thousand men, four hundred were able to bear arms.

3. Cæsar will keep their [1] neighbors from doing [2] harm.

4. The name and nation of the Nervii are reduced [3] almost to destruction.

5. He orders the neighboring people to refrain from doing harm to the Nervii. [4]

Notes. — [1] their: not **suus.** [2] doing : omit. [3] reduced : participle used as an adjective in the neuter plural. [4] Nervii : genitive.

## Chapter XXIX.

1. Limit of Motion : 426, 2, and 427, 2 (258 and b) ; B. 182 ; H. 418 (380 and 2) ; H–B. 385, b, 450, b, 454.

2. Accusative of Duration of Time : 423 (256) ; B. 181 ; H. 417 (379) ; H–B. 387, II.

3. Locative Ablative with Preps. : 429, b (260, b) ; B. 228 ; H. 483 (425, I) ; H–B. 406, 2.

1. They carry all their property into one town.

2. During two days they hold out very bravely.

3. For many years they were harassed by the Gauls.

4. On two sides they have high rocks ; on another, a wall.

5. Leaving six thousand men this side [1] the Rhine, they return [2] home.

Notes. — [1] this side : **cis.** [2] return : commonly **revertor** in the present, **reverti** in the perfect.

## CHAPTER XXX.

1. Ablative of Time *when:* 423 (256); B. 230; H. 486 (429); H–B. 439.

2. Imperfect of Repeated Action : 470 (277) ; B. 260, 2 ; H. 534, 3 (469, II) ; H–B. 484.

3. Perfect of Completed Action : 473 (279) ; B. 262, 3; H. 537, 1, 538, 2 (471, I and 6); H–B. 468, 4, a.

1. On the day of our arrival frequent sallies were made by the enemy from the town.

2. During the first days they taunted us from the walls.

3. At a distance the soldiers made an "agger" and a tower.

4. Then the Aduatuci began to jeer.[1]

5. Can[2] men of such little stature place a tower on our wall?

NOTES. — [1] jeer : two words in Latin.   [2] begin with **num.**

## CHAPTER XXXI.

1. Causal Relative Clauses: 535, e (320, e) ; B. 283, 3 ; H. 592 (517); H–B. 523.

2. Dative with certain Intrans. Verbs: 367 (227) ; B. 187, II, a ; H. 426, 1 (385) ; H–B. 362.

3. Future Conditions less vivid : 516, b (307, b) ; B. 303 ; H. 576, 1 (509, N. 1) ; H–B. 580.

1. They surrender to Cæsar, since he is so powerful.[1]

2. The envoys say the enemy are jealous of their[2] valor.

3. It is better to endure death than slavery.

4. If Cæsar should rob the Aduatuci of their arms,[3] they would be killed.

5. Their enemies would kill them, if they should surrender their arms.

6. It is better to persuade them to give up their arms.

NOTES. — [1] is so powerful : *can so much* (**tantum**).   [2] their : express by the proper form of **suus**.   [3] of their arms : not the genitive.

## CHAPTER XXXII.

1. Ablative of Cause : 404 (245) ; B. 219 ; H. 475 (416) ; H–B. 444.

2. Clauses of Result with **ut (ut nōn)** : 536, 537 (319) ; B. 284 ; H. 570 (500, II) ; H–B. 521, 1, e.

3. Substantive Clauses of Purpose with **ut (nē)** : 563 (331); B. 295, 296; H. 565 (498) ; H–B. 502, 3, a.

1. They order the people to deliver up their arms.

2. Through Cæsar's orders, no wrong will be inflicted.

3. Cæsar spared, according to his custom, those who had surrendered.[1]

4. Cæsar orders the neighbors of the Nervii not to harm them.[2]

5. There is so great a quantity of arms in the town that a third part is concealed.

NOTES. — [1] those who had surrendered : one word in Latin.  [2] them : dative.

## CHAPTER XXXIII.

1. Causal Clauses with **cum** : 549 (326) ; B. 286, 2 ; H. 598 (517) ; H–B. 526.

2. Ablative Absolute : 419 and a (255 and a) ; B. 227 and a ; H. 489 (431, 4) ; H–B. 421.

3. Pass. of Intrans. Verbs used impersonally : 372 (230) ; B. 187, II, b ; H. 518, 1 (465, 1) ; H–B. 364, 2, 292, a.

1. [1] The Aduatuci fought very spiritedly.

2. [1] Thither hasten all the forces of the town.

3. After the shutting [2] of the gates, the townsmen formed a plan.

4. Since they had been driven back, they no longer [3] defended themselves.

5. Now [4] that the town was occupied, the booty was sold.

NOTES. — [1] Use the passive construction. [2] After the shutting : turn in two ways. [8] no longer: nōn iam. [4] Now that the town was occupied : turn in two ways.

## CHAPTER XXXIV.

1. Ablative of Agent with ā (ab): 405 (246); B. 216; H. 468 (415, I); H-B. 406, 1.

2. Accus. and Infin. of Indirect Discourse: 580 (336, 2); B. 314; H. 642 (523, I); H-B. 534, 1, 2.

1. All the maritime states were subdued by Cæsar.

2. Cæsar says that the maritime states have been reduced.

3. At this time P. Crassus had been sent with one legion.

4. Crassus informs Cæsar that one legion has been sent to the Veneti.

5. The Veneti, to whom one legion had been sent, border on the ocean.

## CHAPTER XXXV.

1. Relative Clauses of Purpose: 531, 2 (317, 2); B. 282, 2 and a; H. 589, II (497, I); H-B. 502, 2.

2. Verbs of Promising, Hoping, etc.: 580, c (330, f); H. 614 (535, II); H-B. 593, a.

3. Dative with Certain Adjectives: 384 (234, a); B. 192, 1; H. 434, 2 (391, I); H-B. 362, I-III.

1. The embassies promised to return [1] the next summer.

2. Near the Rhine were many nations of barbarians.

3. These barbarians promised to do Cæsar's bidding.

4. The barbarians send men to give [2] hostages.

5. So great was the joy [8] that a thanksgiving was decreed.

NOTES. — [1] to return: in the Latin idiom, *themselves to be going to return.* [2] to give: put in two ways. [8] joy: **gaudium.**

# VOCABULARIES.

# VOCABULARY.

———•◦•———

If the learner, as often as he refers to this vocabulary for the meaning of a word, will glance over the group of words given in the Etymological Vocabulary under the same root, he will find his knowledge of the relations and meaning of words, and consequently his power to read Latin, rapidly increase.

**Ā** or **Ab** (**abs**), prep. w. abl. [APA-], *from, away from,* 6, 13, 18, 24, 25; *at the hands of,* 31, 33; *away, at a distance of,* 7, 30; *in, on, at,* 23, 25; *by,* 1, 5, 9, etc.

**Ab·dŏ, 3,** -didī, -ditum [2 DA-], *put away; hide,* 19.

**Ab·sum,** -esse, āfuī [ES-], *be away from,* 11; *be distant,* 4, 5, 6, 13, 16, 17, 21; *with ā or ab and abl.*

**Āc,** see **At·que.**

**Ac·cēdŏ** (**adc-**), **3,** -cessī, -cessum [CAD-], *go towards, approach,* 13, w. ad and acc.; *arise, increase in,* 7, with dat.

**Ac·cidŏ** (**adc-**), **3,** -cidī, ——— [CAD-], *fall to* or *towards; befall, happen,* 35; w. dat. Cf. incidō, ēveniō.

**Ac·cipiŏ** (**adc-**), **3,** -cēpī, -ceptum [CAP-], *take to one's self; accept,* 15; *receive,* 13; *suffer,* 33.

**Acervus,** -ī, M. [1 AC-], *thing brought to a point; pile, heap,* 32.

**Aciēs,** ēī- (-ē, 23), F. [1 AC-], *edge; line of battle, army,* 8, 9, 19, 20, 23, 25.

**Ācor·iter,** adv. [1 AC-], *sharply; fiercely, desperately,* 10, 33.

**Ad,** prep. w. acc., *to, towards,* 8, 13, 28, etc.; *up to,* 17; *near,* 4, 19, 21, 33; *for,* 1, 4, 8, 21, etc.; *after, according to,* 31.

**Ad·aequŏ, 1** [IC-, AIC-], *make equal to, equal,* 32.

**Ad·clīvis** (**acc-**), -e, adj. [CLĪ-], *sloping upward,* 29. Cf. dēclīvis.

**Ad·clīvitās** (**acc-**), -ātis, F. [CLĪ-], *upward slope, rise,* 18. Cf. dēclīvitās, dēiectus.

**Ad·com·modŏ** (**acconm-**), **1** [2 MA-, MAD-], *fit* or *adapt to; put on,* 21. Cf. induō.

**Ad·dūcŏ, 3,** -dūxī, -ductum [DVC-], *lead* or *bring to,* 5; *lead up,* 1; w. ad and acc.

**Ad·eŏ,** -īre, -iī, -itum [1 I-], *go to; reach, get at,* 7.

**Ad·ferŏ** (**aff-**), -ferre, attulī, allātum [1 FER-], *bring* or *carry to,* 1.

**Ad·finitās** (aff-), -ātis, f. [2 FID-], *relationship by marriage,* 4. Cf. propinquitās.

**Ad·gredior** (agg-), **3**, -gressus [GRAD-], *go to, approach; attack,* 9, 10. Cf. adorior.

**Ad·iciō, 3,** -iēcī, -iectum [IA-, IAC-], *throw to* or *against; hurl, cast,* 21.

**Ad·itus,** -ūs, m. [1 I-, AI-], *going to, approach,* 16, 29 ; *access, admittance,* 15.

**Ad·iuvō, 1,** -iūvī, -iūtum [DIV-, DI-, DIAV-], *help, aid,* 17.

**Ad·ministrō, 1** [2 MAN-, MI-], *put the hand to ; attend to,* 20, 22.

**Ad·orior, 4,** -ortus [OL-, OR-], *rise up against; attack,* 11, 17. Cf. adgredior.

**Ad·propinquō** (app-), **1** [PARC-, PLEC-], *come near to, approach,* 10, 31, w. dat. ; 19, w. ad and acc. Cf. subeō, succēdō.

**Aduātucī,** -ōrum, m., *tribe, originally German, in Belgian Gaul, on left bank of the Maas,* 4, 16, 29, 31.

**Ad·ventus,** -ūs, m. [BA-, VA-, VEN-], *coming to* or *drawing near; approach, arrival,* 7, 16, 25, 27, 30. Cf. successus, aditus.

**Ad·versus,** -a, -um, adj. (P. of advertō) [VERT-], *turned to* or *towards; opposite, in the face,* 8, 18, 24 ; *adversō colle, up hill,* 19 ; w. dat.

**Aedi·ficium,** -ī, n. [AID- ; FAC-], *building,* 7.

**Aeduī,** -ōrum, m., *powerful Celtic people between upper courses of Loire and Seine,* 5, 10, 14, 15.

**Aeduus,** -a, -um, adj., *Aeduan,* 5, 14.

**Aegrē,** adv., *with regret* or *displeasure ; barely, with difficulty,* 6.

**Aequāl·iter,** adv. [IC-, AIC-], *evenly,* 18.

**Aestās,** -ātis, f. [AID-], *burning season; summer,* 2, 35.

**Aestuārium,** -ī, n. [AID-], *pertaining to rolling; inlet, sea-marsh,* 28.

**Aetās,** -ātis, f. [1 I-, AI-], *age, old age,* 16.

**Ager,** -grī, m. [AG-], *cultivated land ; land, field,* 4, 5, 7, 9.

**Ag·ger,** -eris, m. [GER-], *that which is brought to a place,* i.e. *materials for a mound,* 20 ; *mound, rampart,* 12, 30, 32.

**Āgmen,** -inis, n. [AG-], *that which is set in motion ; marching column,* 11, 17, 19, 23, 26.

**Agō, 3,** ēgī, āctum [AG-], *put in motion ; bring up,* 12, 30 ; *take along,* 29 ; *carry on, do,* 20.

**Aliās,** adv. (acc. pl. f. of alius) [2 AL- (ALI-)], *at another time; aliās . . . aliās, at one time . . . at another,* 29.

**Aliēnus,** -a, -um, adj. [2 AL-, (ALI-)], *belonging to another, another's,* 10.

**Al·iter,** adv. [2 AL-], *otherwise, in another manner,* 19.

**Alius,** -a, -ud, adj., gen. alīus [2 AL- (ALI-)], *other, another, different,* 20, 22, 23, 24, 26, 31.

**Alter,** -era, -erum, adj., gen. -ius [2 AL-], *other (of two),* 5, 21 ; *alter . . . alter, the one . . . the other.*

**Altitūdō,** -inis, F. [1 AL-], *elevation, height,* 5, 12, 18, 31, 32.

**Altus,** -a, -um, adj. [1 AL-], *become great by nourishment; lofty, high,* 27, 29.

**Ambiānī,** -ōrum, M., *Belgian tribe near modern Amiens,* 4, 15.

**Amīcitia,** -ae, F. [AM-], *friendship,* 14.

**Ā·mittō,** 3, -mīsī, -missum [MIT-], *let go from one's self; lose,* 25.

**Amplī·ficō,** 1 [PLE-, PLO-; FAC-], *make larger, increase,* 14.

**Am·plius,** adv. (N. compar. of amplus) [ambi- ; PLE-, PLO-], *more,* 7, 16, 29.

**Andocumborius,** -ī, M., *man of high rank among the Remi,* 3.

**Andēs,** -ium, M., *tribe of Gaul north of the Loire, modern Anjou,* 35.

**Angustus,** -a, -um, adj., *contracted; narrow, difficult;* **in angustō,** *in a critical state,* 25.

**Animus,** -ī, M. [AN-], *soul; mind, feelings,* 21 ; *spirit, courage,* 15, 21, 25, 27 ; *character,* 1.

**Annus,** -ī, M., *that which goes round ; year,* 29.

**Ante,** [ANT-], *before;* as adv., =anteā, *before, formerly,* 12, 22, 33 ; as prep. w. acc., *before* (of time), 35 ; (of place), 32.

**Antīquitus,** adv. [ANT-], *from ancient times; in olden times,* 4 ; *from of old,* 17.

**A·pertus,** -a, -um, adj. (P. of aperiō) [2 PAR-, POR-], *without covering ; open, unobstructed,* 18, 19 ; *uncovered, exposed,* 23.

**Ap·pellō** **(adp-),** 1 [PAL-, PEL-], *bring one's self to a person ; accost, address,* 25 ; *call,* 4.

**Ap·ud,** prep. w. acc. [APA-], *near, among,* 2, 4, 7, 14.

**Ar·bitror,** 1 [BA-, VA-], *be a hearer* or *spectator, think, suppose, believe,* 4, 28 ; w. acc. and inf.

**Arbor,** -oris, F. [1 AL-, AR-], *tree,* 17.

**Ar·cessō,** 3, -īvī, -ītum [CAD-], *cause to come to ; summon, send for,* 20.

**Arduus,** -a, -um, adj. [1 AL-, AR-, strengthened to ARDH-], *steep,* 33.

**Ariēs,** -etis, M., *battering-ram,* 32.

**Arma,** -ōrum, N. [AR-], *things adapted ; arms, weapons,* 3, 4, 9, 13, etc.

**Armātūra,** -ae, F. [AR-], *arming ; equipment,* 10, 24.

**Armō,** 1 [AR-], *furnish with arms ; arm, equip,* 4, 27.

**A·scendō** **(adsc-),** 3, -dī, -scēnsum [SCAND-], *mount up, climb,* 27.

**A·scēnsus** **(adsc-),** -ūs, M. [SCAND-], *ascending ; ascent, way up,* 33.

**At,** conj., *but, on the other hand,* 23, 27.

**At·que** (before vowels and consonants), **āc** (before consonants only), *and also, and especially, and,* 3, 5, 6, etc. ; *as,* 6 ; *than,* 19. Cf. et and -que.

**Atrebatēs,** -um, M., *Belgian people in the region of modern Arras,* 4, 16, 23.

**At·tingō** (adt-), **3,** -tigī, -tāctum, [TAG-], *touch against; approach, reach,* 32 ; *border upon,* 15, 34.

**Auctōritās,** -ātis, F. [AVG-], *power, standing, influence,* 4, 14, 15.

**Audāc·ter,** adv. [1 AV-], *boldly,* 10, 26.

**Audeō, 2,** ausus [1 AV-], *venture, dare,* 8, 17, 19, 27 ; w. complementary infin.

**Audiō, 4** [2 AV-], *listen to ; hear, hear about,* 12, 31, w. acc. ; 12, w. acc. and infin.

**Aulercī,** -ōrum, M., *tribe in Bretagne and Normandy,* 34.

**Aurunculēius,** -ī, M., *L. A. Cotta, lieutenant of Cæsar,* 11.

**Au·t,** conj. [2 TA-], *or* (excluding the other), 30, 33 ; aut . . . aut, *either . . . or,* 25.

**Au·tem,** postpositive conj. [2 TA-], *but, on the other hand,* 9 ; *moreover,* 19.

**Auxilium,** -ī, N. [AVG-], *aid, support, assistance,* 10, 24, 29 ; pl. *auxiliary forces,* 14. Cf. subsidium.

**Á·vertō, 3,** -tī, -sum [VERT-], *turn away from.* Aversī, see note, 26.

**Axona,** -ae, F., *river in country of the Belgæ,* 5, 9.

### B.

**Baculus,** -ī, M., P. Sextius B., *centurion,* 25.

**Baleāris,** -e, adj., *Balearic, of the Balearic Islands,* 7.

**Barbarus,** -a, -um, adj., *foreign, non-Roman,* 35.

**Belgae,** -ārum, M., *collective name of tribes living in the country bounded by the Seine, Marne, Moselle, Rhine, and the ocean,* 1, 2, 3, following.

**Bellovacī,** -ōrum, M., *strongest tribe of the Belgæ, north of the Seine and on right bank of the Oise and Somme,* 4, 5, 10, 13, 14.

**Bellum,** -ī, N. [DVA-, DVI-], *contest between two ; war,* 4, 9, 14, 16, 29, 31, 35.

**Bibrax,** -ctis, F. (N.?), *town of the Remi,* 6.

**Boduōgnātus,** -ī, M., *leader of the Nervii,* 23.

**Bratuspantium,** -ī, N., *chief town of the Bellovaci,* 13.

**Brevitās,** -ātis, F., *shortness, brevity,* 20, 30. Cf. exiguitās.

**Britannia,** -ae, F., *Britain,* 4, 14.

### C.

**Cadāver,** -eris, N. [CAD-], *that which falls down dead ; dead body,* 27.

**Cadō, 3,** cecidī, cāsum [CAD-], *fall,* 27.

**Caeroesī,** -ōrum, M., *German tribe in Belgian Gaul,* 4.

**Caesar,** -aris, M., *Gaius Julius Cæsar, conqueror of Gaul and author of the Commentaries,* 1, 2, 5, etc.

**Calamitās,** -ātis, F. [SCAL-], *injury, disaster,* 14, 28.

**Caletī,** -ōrum (-ēs, -um), M., *tribe in Normandy, on the Seine,* 4.

Cālō, -ōnis, M., *groom, soldier's servant,* 24, 26, 27.

Captīvus, -a, -um, adj. [CAP-], *taken prisoner; captive,* 16, 17.

Caput, -itis, N. [CAP-], *head; individual, person,* 33.

Carnūtēs, -um, M., *important Gallic tribe between the Loire and Seine rivers,* 35.

Castellum, -ī, N. dim. [SCAD-, CAD-], *redoubt, stronghold,* 8, 9, 29, 30, 33.

Castra, -ōrum, N. [SCAD-, CAD-], *camp,* 2, 5, 6, etc.

Cāsus, -ūs, M. [CAD-], *falling; happening; chance,* 21; *misfortune,* 31.

Causa, -ae, F. [CAV-], *cause, reason,* 1, 7, 10, 11; causā, used like prep. post-positive, *for the sake of, for the purpose of,* 10, 15, 17, 20, 21, 24.

Cēdō, 3, cessī, cessum [CAD-], *go; fall back; give way, retreat,* 19.

Celeritās, -ātis, F. [CEL-], *swiftness, quickness,* 12, 19, 20, 26, 31.

Celer·iter, adv. [CEL-], *swiftly, quickly, promptly,* 3, 12, 23, 33.

Cēlō, 1 [2 CAL-, SCAL-], *hide, conceal,* 32, 33.

Centum, num. adj. indeclin. [CEN-], *hundred,* 4.

Centuriō, -ōnis, M. [CEN-], *commander of a century, centurion, captain,* 17, 25.

Certus, -a, -um, adj. [2 CER-, CRE-], *determined; definite,* 11; *certain, regular,* 22; certiōrem facere, *inform,* 1, 2, 10, 34; w. acc. and infin.

Cēterī, -ōrum, pl. adj. [CA-, CI-], *the others, rest,* 3. Cf. reliquī.

Cimbrī, -ōrum, M., *German tribe which invaded Gaul and the Province in the second century,* 4, 29.

Circī·ter, adv. [CVR-, CIR-; 1 I-], *going in a circle; about, not far from,* 2, 8, 13, 18, 32.

Circu·itus, -ūs, M. [CVR-, CIR-; 1 I-], *going in a circle; circumference,* 29, 30.

Circum-, prep. w. acc. [CVR-, CIR-], *around, about;* here only in composition.

Circum·iciō, 3, -iēcī, -iectum [IA-, IAC-], *throw around; place around,* 6.

Circum·mūniō, 4, [2 MV-], *wall up around; blockade,* 30.

Circum·veniō, 4, -vēnī, -ventum [BA-, VA-, VEN-], *come around; surround, outflank,* 8, 10, 23, 24, 26.

Cis, prep. w. acc. [CA-, CI-], *on this side, this side of,* 3.

Citerior, -us, -ōris, adj. [CA-, CI-], *more on this side; hither, nearer,* 1, 2.

Citrā, prep. w. acc. [CA-, CI-], *on this side, this side of,* 29. Cf. cis.

Cīvitās, -ātis, F. *citizenship; community,* 3, 4, 5, etc.

Clāmor, -ōris, M. [1 CAL-], *loud call; shouting,* 11, 24.

Claudō, 3, -sī, -sum, *shut, close,* 33; *close, bring up,* 19.

Clē·mentia, -ae, F. [CLĪ-; 1 MAN-, MEN-], *indulgent disposition; gentleness, mildness,* 14, 31.

Co·acervō, 1 [1 AC-], *heap up,* 27.

Co · epī, -isse, -ptus (defective verb, with tenses from present stem lacking) [AP-, OP-], *have begun, began,* 5, 6, 10, 12, 13, 19, 23, 26.

Cŏ · gnŏscŏ, 3, -gnōvī, -gnitum [GNA-, GNO-], *understand thoroughly ;· perceive, learn, ascertain,* 2, 5, 11, 17, w. acc. and inf. ; 4, 26, w. indir. question ; plperf. *knew,* 10.

Cŏ · gŏ, 3, -ēgī, -āctum [AG-], *drive together, compel ; gather, rally,* 2, 5. Cf. condūcō.

Co · hors, -hortis, F., *multitude enclosed : cohort,* 5, 25.

Co · hortātiŏ, -ōnis, F., *cheering on, urging, encouraging, appeal to,* 25.

Co · hortor, 1, *cheer on, urge, call upon,* 5, 20, 21, 25, w. acc. ; 21 foll. by clause w. ut.

Collis, -is, M., *hill,* 8, 18, 19, 22.

Com · meātus (conm-), -ūs, M., *going to and fro ; train of supplies, provisions,* 5, 9.

Com · ĕs, -itis, M., *comrade.*

Com · memorŏ (conm-), 1 [1 SMAR-, MAR-], *keep in mind ; mention, relate,* 28.

Com · mittŏ (conm-), 3, -mīsī, -mīssum [MIT-], *cause to go together ; join,* 19, 21.

Com · modē (conm-), adv. [2 MA-, MAD-], *duly, aptly ; easily, advantageously,* 20.

Com · moveŏ (conm-), 2, -mōvī, -mōtum [1 MV-, MOV-], *move violently ; startle, alarm, make anxious,* 2, 31.

Com · mūnis (conm-), -e, adj. [2 MV-], *serving together ; common, general,* 4, 5.

Com · mūtātiŏ (conm-), -ōnis, F. [1 MV-, MOV-], *change,* 27.

Com · parŏ (conp-), 1 [2 PAR-, POR-], *bring* or *put together ; get ready, provide, procure,* 2, 12.

Com · pellŏ (conp-), 3, -pulī, -pulsum [PAL-, PEL-], *drive together, gather ; drive in a body, rout,* 23.

Com · ploŏ (conp-), 2, -ēvī, -ētum [PLE-, PLO-], *fill completely ; fill,* 24.

Com · plūrēs (conp-), -a (-ia), gen. -ium, adj. [PLE-, PLO-, PLV-], *several together, a large number,* 17.

Con-, for scom- = cum [SEC-], *with, together ;* in composition, denoting completeness or union ; sometimes intensive.

Con · cīdŏ, 3, -cīdī, -cīsum [2 SAC-, SEC-, SCĪD-], *cut up entirely ; cut to pieces, destroy,* 11.

Con · cilium, -ī, N. [1 CAL-], *that which is called together ; meeting, assembly,* 4, 10.

Con · currŏ, 3, -currī or -cucurrī, -cursum [CEL-, CER-], *run together ; hurry, rally, gather,* 20, 33.

Con · diciŏ, -ōnis, F., [DĬC-, DIC], *talking together ; agreement, stipulation, terms,* 15, 32.

Condrūsī, -ōrum, M., *Belgic tribe on the Meuse,* 4.

Con · dūcŏ, 3, -dūxī, -ductum [DVC-], *lead together ; collect, muster,* 2 ; *hire,* 1.

Cōn · ferŏ, -ferre, -tulī, -lātum [1 FER-], *bring* or *bear together ; gather, collect,* 15, 25, 29 ; with reflex. pronoun, *betake one's self, go,* 13.

Cŏn·fertus, -a, -um, adj. (P. of cōn·ferciō), *pressed together; compact, in close array*, 23; *crowded together*, 25.

ᵒŏn·ficiŏ, 3, -fēcī, -fectum [FAC-], *make completely; perform, accomplish*, 12; *raise, put in the field*, 4; *exhaust, wear out*, 23, 25, 27.

Cŏn·fīdŏ, 3, -fīsus sum [1 FID-, FĪD-], *trust entirely; believe, trust firmly*, 30, w. acc. and infin.

Cŏn·firmŏ, 1 [2 FER-], *make firm; give assurance, pledge one's self*, 15, w. acc. and infin.; *encourage, reassure*, 19; *confirm*, 11.

Cŏn·flīgŏ, 3, -xī, -ctum [FLAG-, FLIG-], *strike or dash together; contend, fight*, 5; w. cum and abl.

Con·gredior, 3, -gressus [GRAD-], *step together; meet, have an engagement with, fight*, 23. Cf. cōnflīgō, pūgnō.

Cŏn·iciŏ, 3, -iēcī, -iectum [IA-, IAC-], *throw together; hurl*, 6, 27; *drive, rout*, 23; *place hastily*, 16, 28. Cf. compellō.

Con·iungŏ, 3, -iūnxī, -iūnctum [IV- IVG-], *draw together, join*, 3, 4, 26.

Con·iūrŏ, 1 [IV-, IVG-], *swear together; make a sworn agreement, conspire*, 1, 3.

Con·locŏ (coll-), 1, *place, station, set*, 8, 19, 22, 29, 30.

Cŏnor, 1, *undertake, attempt*, 9, 10, 12, 23.

Cŏn·sanguineus, -a, -um, adj., *possessing the same blood; kindred*, 3.

Cŏn·scrībŏ, 3, -psi, -ptum [SCARP-], *write together* (in a list); *enroll, enlist*, 2, 8, 19.

Cŏn·sēnsus, -ūs, м. [SENT-], *agreement, harmony, concerted action*, 28, 29.

Cŏn·sentiŏ, 4, -sēnsī, -sēnsum [SENT-], *feel with*, 3; *join hands* (*with*), *make common cause with*, 3; w. cum and abl.

Cŏn·sequor, 3, -secūtus [SEC-], *follow thoroughly; attain, obtain*, 1.

Cŏn·servŏ, 1 [SAL-, SER-], *keep thoroughly; preserve, save, spare*, 12, 15, 28, 31, 32.

Cŏn·sīdŏ, 3, -sēdī, -sessum [SED-, SID-], *sit down together; settle, take position*, 4, 16.

Cŏn·silium, -ī, N., *consultation; design, plan of action*, 9, 14, 33; *advice, suggestion*, 17.

Cŏn·similis, -e, adj., [2 SA-, SIM-], *altogether like, quite similar*, 11; w. dat.

Cŏn·sistŏ, 3, -stitī, — [STA-], *make stand; take position, stand*, 6, 23, 26; *make a stand, rally*, 11, 17, 21; *depend upon, be based on*, 33.

Cŏn·spectus, -ūs, м. [SPEC-], *view, sight*, 25.

Cŏn·spiciŏ, 3, -spēxī, -spectum [SPEC-], *look at with attention; behold, catch sight of, see*, 21, 26, w. acc.; 24, w. acc. and infin.

Cŏn·spicor, 1 [SPEC-], *get a sight of, espy, observe*, 26, 27. Cf. cōnspiciō.

Cŏn·stanter, adv. [STA-], *standing firm; uniformly*, 2.

Cōn·stituō, 3, -uī, -ūtum [STA-], place together; determine, appoint, fix, 11; set up, place, 12, 30; station, 8, 19; decide, 10, w. acc. and infin. Cf. statuō.

Cōn·suēscō, 3, -suēvī, -suētum [SOVO-, SVO-], accustom; become accustomed; pf. be accustomed (= solēre), 14, 31.

Cōn·suētūdō, -inis, F. [SOVO-, SVO-], custom, habit, 17, 19, 32. Cf. mōs.

Con·temptus, -ūs, M. [TEM-], scorn, contempt, 30.

Con·tendō, 3, -dī, -ntum [1 TA-, TEN-], strain with all one's might; march, push on, hasten, 7, 9, 10, 12, 19, 23, 24; struggle, contend, 9, 13, 30.

Con·tineō, 2, -uī, -tentum [1 TA-, TEN-], hold or keep together; restrain, hold back, 11; keep, 11, 18, 30.

Con·trā, adv. [SEC-], against, on the other hand, 17; as prep., w. acc., 1, 3, 13, 33.

Con·trārius, -a, -um, adj. [SEC-], situated over against, opposite, 18; w. dat.

Con·tumēlia, -ae, F. [TEM-], great swelling; disgrace, insult, 14.

Con·veniō, 4, -vēnī, -ventum [BA-, VA·-, VEN-], come together, meet, 5, 10, 12; impersonal, be agreed upon, 19.

Convertō, 3, -tī, -sum [VERT-], wholly turn; turn around, turn, direct, 26.

Con·vocō, 1 [VOC-], call together, summon, 10.

C·ōpia, -ae, F. [AP-, OP-], ability; ample supply, supply, 2; pl., resources, supplies, 10; forces, troops, 5, 7, 8, etc.

Cornū, -ūs, N. [CAR-], horn; wing of an army, 23, 25.

Corpus, -oris, N. [1 CER-, CRE-], what is made; body, 30; corpse, 10, 27.

Cortex, -icis, M. and F. [CAR-], part that splits off; bark, 33.

Cotī·diē, adv. [CA-; DIV-, DI-], on every day; daily, regularly, 8.

Cotta, -ae, M., L. Arunculeius, one of Cæsar's lieutenants, 11.

Crassus, -ī, M., P. Licinius, one of Cæsar's lieutenants, 34.

Crēber, -bra, -brum, adj. [1 CER-, CRE-], made to increase; thick, numerous, frequent, 1, 17, 30.

Crēdō, 3, -didī, -ditum [CRAT-; 2 DA-], put trust in; believe, 33, w. acc. and infin. Cf. cōnfīdō.

Crēs, -ētis, M., Cretan, 7.

Cruciātus, -ūs, M. [CVR-, CIR-], torture, 31.

Cum, prep. w. abl. [SEC-], with, in company with, together with, 3, 10, 13, etc.; at same time with, 5, 7, 16; with, provided with, 11, 33.

Cum, conj. [CA-, CI-], temporal, when, 1, 4, 6, 8, following; cum prīmum, as soon as, 2; causal, as, since, 11, 17, 22, etc.; concessive, although, while, 29; cum . . . tum, both . . . and, 4.

C·ūnctus, -a, -um, adj. [IV-, IVG-], all together; all, entire, 29.

Cupiō, 3, -īvī, -ītum, desire eagerly, be eager, 25.

**Curiosolitēs**, -um, M. (acc. -ēs, -ās), *people of Armoric Gaul*, 34.

**Cursus**, -ūs, M. [CEL-, CER-], *running, speed*, 23, 26.

**Custōdia**, -ae, F. [SCV-, CV-], *guard-keeping; guard, protection*, 29.

**D.**

**Dē**, prep. w. abl., *from; down from*, 32 ; of time, *in, about*, 7 ; *for, on account of*, 7 ; *for, about, concerning*, 2, 4, 6, etc.

**Dē·beō** [for dehibeō], **2**, -uī, -itum [HAB-], *have from;* impersonal, *owe, ought*, 27, 33.

**Decem**, num. adj. indecl. [DEC-], *ten*, 4.

**Dē·cernō**, **3**, -crēvī, -crētum [2 CER-, CRE-], *decide; decide upon, decree*, 35.

**Dē·certō**, **1** [2 CER-], *fight a decisive battle*, 10. Cf. cōnflīgō, congredior, dīmicō, pūgnō.

**Decimus**, -a, -um, adj. [DEC-], *tenth*, 21, 23, 25, 26.

**Dē·clīvis**, -e, adj. [CLĪ-], *inclining down-hill, sloping*, 18.

**Decumānus** (deci-), -a, -um, adj. [DEC-], *of the tenth cohort*, in the phrase, decumāna porta, *rear gate*, 24, main entrance to a Roman camp.

**Dē·currō**, **3**, -cucurrī or -currī, -cursum [CEL-, CER-], *run down*, 19, 21.

**Dē·ditīcius**, -a, -um, adj. [1 DA-], *one who has surrendered;* as noun, M., *prisoner of war*, 17 ; *subjects*, 32.

**Dē·ditiō**, -ōnis, F. [1 DA-], *giving one's self up; surrender*, 12, 13, 32, 33.

**Dē·dō**, **3**, -didī, -ditum [1 DA-], *give up* or *away; surrender*, 15, 28, 32.

**Dē·dūcō**, **3**, -xī, -ductum [DVC-], *lead away, bring off*, 2, 33, 35 ; *bring (to)*, 10, 31. Cf. redigō.

**Dē·fendō**, **3**, -dī, -fēnsum [FEN-, FEND-], *thrust away; repel*, 29 ; *defend*, 10, 12, 31, 33.

**Dē·fēnsiō**, -ōnis, F. [FEN-, FEND-], *protection, defence*, 7.

**Dē·fēnsor**, -ōris, M. [FEN-, FEND-], *defender*, 6, 12.

**Dē·ferō**, -ferre, -tulī, -lātum [1 FER-], *bear* or *bring away; bear, report*, 17, 19 ; *bestow*, 4 ; w. ad and acc.

**Dē·ficiō**, **3**, -fēcī, -fectum [FAC-], *make from; give out, fail*, 10 ; *revolt (from), forsake, desert*, 14 ; w. ab and abl.

**Dē·iciō**, **3**, -iēcī, -iectum [IA-, IAC-], *hurl down; drive away, dislodge*, 27.

**Dē·iectus**, -ūs, M. [IA-, IAC-], *slope, declivity*, 8, 22. Cf. dēclīvis, adclīvis.

**De·inde**, adv. [2 I-], *from here; thereupon, then, in the next place*, 1.

**Dē·leō**, **2**, -ēvī, -ētum [LI-], *wipe out, destroy*, 27.

**Dē·ligō**, **3**, -lēgī, -lēctum [1 LEG-, LIG-], *choose out; choose, select*, 17, 18, 29. Cf. ēligō.

**Dē·mōnstrō**, **1** [1 MAN-, MEN-], *point out, explain, mention*, 1, 9, 22 ; w. acc. and infin., 17.

**Dēnique**, adv., *and thereupon, finally; at any rate, at least*, 33.

**Dēnsus**, -a, -um, adj., *thick, dense, close*, 22.

**Dē·pōnō**, 3, -posuī, -positum [1 SA-, SI-], *put aside* or *down; lay aside, place in safety*, 29.

**Dē·populor**, 1 [SCAL-, SPOL-], *lay waste, ravage*, 7.

**Dē·precor**, 1 [PREC-], *avert by praying; petition against, pray to be spared*, 31.

**Dē·serō**, 3, -uī, -tum [1 SER-, SVAR-], *undo, sever connection with; abandon, desert*, 25, 29.

**Dē·sistō**, 3, -stitī, — [STA-], *remove from; cease, stop*, 11.

**Dē·spectus**, -ūs, M. [SPEC-], *looking down upon; opportunity for distant views, prospect*, 29.

**Dē·spērō**, 1 [SPA-, PA-], *give up hope; despair of*, 24.

**Dē·spoliō**, 1 [SCAL-, SPOL-], *rob, deprive*, 31; w. acc. and abl.

**Dē·sum**, -esse, -fuī [ES-], *be away; be lacking, fail*, 21. Cf. dēficiō.

**Dē·terreō**, 2, -uī, -itum [TER-, TERS-], *frighten from; prevent, deter*, 8.

**Dē·trahō**, 3, -xī, -ctum, *drag from; take from, remove*, 25.

**Dē·trūdō**, 3, -sī, -sum, *thrust away; remove*, 21. Cf. dētrahō.

**Dē·veniō**. 4, -vēnī, -ventum [BA-, VA-, VEN-], *come down into; come to, reach*, 21; w. prep. and acc. Cf. adpropīnquō.

**Dexter**, -tra, -trum, adj, *right, on the right hand*, 23, 25.

(**Diciō**), -ōnis, F., no nom. [DIC-, DIC-], *sway, control*, 34.

**Dīcō**, 3, -xī, -ctum [DĪC-, DIC-], *point out by speaking; say, state, mention*, 1, 3, 4, etc.; w. acc. and infin.

**Diēs**, -ēī, M. and F. [DIV-, DI-], *day*, 2, 5, 6, etc.

**Dif·ficilis** (disf-), -e, adj. [FAC-], *not to be done; difficult, hard*, 27.

**Dif·ficultās** (disf-), -ātis, F. [FAC-], *difficulty, strait, trouble*, 20.

**Dī·ligen·ter**, adv. [1 LEG-, LIG-], *attentively, scrupulously, with painstaking*, 5, 28.

**Dī·mētior**, 4, -mēnsus [1 MA-, MAN-], *measure off; stake off, lay out, survey*, 19.

**Dī·micō**, 1, *move rapidly back and forth; fight, contend*, 21. Cf. cōnflīgō, congredior, contendō.

**Dī·mittō**, 3, -mīsī, mīssum [MIT-], *send out in different directions, despatch*, 5, 14, 21.

**Dī·ripiō**, 3, -uī, -reptum [RAP-, RVP-], *tear in pieces; sack, plunder*, 17.

**Dis·cēdō**, 3, -cessī, -cessum [CAD-], *go apart; go away, depart*, 7, 11, 20.

**Dis·cessus**, -ūs, M. [CAD-], *departure, withdrawal*, 14.

**Dis·sipō**, 1, *scatter, break up*, 24.

**Dis·tineō**, 2, -uī, -tentum [1 TA-, TEN-], *keep apart; prevent union of, separate*, 5.

**Diū**, adv. [DIV-, DI-], *by day; for a long time, long;* compar. diūtius, 1, 6, 10.

Dī·versus, -a, -um. adj. (P. of dīvertō) [VERT-], *turned away from; facing in different directions*, 22 ; *different*, 23 ; *separated*, 24.

Dīvīnus, -a, -um, adj. [DIV-, DI-], *of the gods, divine*, 31.

Divitiacus, -ī, M., *leader of the Ædui, brother of Dumnorix*, 5, 10, 14, 15 ; *chieftain of the Suessiones*, 4.

Dō, dare, dedī, datum [1 DA-], *give*, 2, 3, 20, 21, 35 ; inter sē, *exchange*, ·1.

Doceō, 2, -uī, -ctum [DIC-, DAC- (DOC-)], *show, teach, explain*, 5, 20.

Domesticus, -a,-um, adj. [DOM-], *of home, native, own*, 10.

Domi·cilium, -ī, N. [DOM- ; 2 CAL-, SCAL-], *dwelling-place*, 29.

Dominor, 1, *lord it, be master*, 31.

Domus, -ūs, F. [DOM-], *home*, 10, 11, 24, 29.

Du·bitō, 1 [DVA- ; BA-], *go to and fro ; doubt, hesitate*, 2, 23.

Du·centī, -ae, -a, num. adj. [DVA-, DVI- ; CEN-], *two hundred*, 18, 29.

Dūcō, 3, -xī, ductum [DVC-], *lead, conduct*, 8, 12, 13, 19.

Dum [for dium], adv. [DIV-, DI-], *while*.

Duo, -ae, -o, num. adj. [DVA-, DVI-], *two*, 2, 7, 8, 9, etc.

Duo·decimus, -a, -um, adj. [DVA-, DVI- ; DEC-], *twelfth*, 23, 25.

Duo·dē·vīgintī, num. adj. indecl. [DVA-, DVI-], *eighteen*, 5.

Du·plex, -icis, adj. [DVA-, PARC-, PLEC-], *twofold, double*, 29.

Dux, -cis, M. [DVC-], *leader*, 23 ; *guide*, 7.

**E.**

Ē or Ex, prep. w. abl., *from, out of*, 3, 6, 13, etc.; *after*, 6 ; *on*, 8 ; *in consequence of*, 35.

Eburōnēs, -um, M., *Belgian people near the Rhine*, 4.

Ē·ditus, -a, -um, adj. (P. of ēdō) [1 DA-], *set forth ; elevated, rising*, 8.

Ē·dūcō, 3, -xī, -ductum [DVC-], *lead out, lead forth*, 8.

Ef·ficiō (ect-), 3, -fēcī, -fectum [FAC-], *work out ; bring about, effect*, 5, 17 ; w. ut and subj.

Ē·gredior, 3, -gressus [GRAD-], *go out ; sally forth*, 24 ; *depart from, go forth*, 11, 13.

Ē·gregiē, adv., *out of the flock ; remarkably, excellently*, 29.

Ē·ligō, 3, -lēgī, -lēctum [1 LEG-, LIG-], *choose out ; pick from, choose*, 4. Cf. dēligo.

Ē·mittō, 3, -mīsī, -missum [MIT-], *send out ; hurl, let fly*, 23.

Emō, 3, ēmī, ēmptum [EM-], *take in exchange ; buy*, 33.

Ē·nāscor, 3, -nātus [GEN-, GN-, GNA-], *grow out, spring up ; sprout forth*, 17.

Enim, co-ord. conj., post-positive, *for, in fact*, 17. Cf. nam.

Eō, adv. (old dat. or abl. N. of is) [2 I-], *there, thither*, 3, 5, 25, 33.

**Equĕs,** -itis, M. [2 AC-], *horseman, cavalry-man, knight,* 9, 18, 19, 24, 26, 27.

**Equester,** -tris, -tre, adj. [2 AC-], *of horsemen, cavalry,* 8, 9.

**Equitātus,** -ūs, M. [2 AC-], *riding; cavalry,* 10, 11, 17, 19.

**Ergō,** *because of; therefore.*

**Ē · ruptiō,** -ōnis, F. [RAP-, RVP-], *bursting forth; sally,* 33.

**Esuviī,** -ōrum, M., *people·in Normandy,* 34.

**Et,** co-ord. conj. *and,* 1, 2, 3, etc.; et . . . et, *both* . . . *and,* 3, 4, 5, etc.

**Et · iam,** adv. and conj. *and now; also,* 1, 4, 14, 16, 17, 21; *even, still,* 4, 25, 27.

**Ē · ventus,** -ūs, M. [BA-, VA-, VEN-], *coming forth; outcome, issue, result,* 22.

**Ex,** see **Ē.**

**Ex · agitō, 1** [AG-], *disturb, harass,* 29.

**Ex · animō, 1** [AN-], *deprive of life; make breathless,* 23.

**Ex · audiō, 4** [2 AV-], *hear distinctly; hear from a distance,* 11.

**Ex · cēdō, 3,** -cessī, -cessum [CAD-], *go out; withdraw, go away,* 25.

**Ex · cursiō,** -ōnis, F. [CEL-, CER-], *running forth; sally,* 30. Cf. ēruptiō.

**Ex · eō,** -īre, -iī, -itum· [1 I-], *go out; withdraw,* 33. Cf. excēdō.

**Ex · ercitō, 1** [ARC-] (*drive out of the enclosure*), *keep busy; train, drill,* 20.

**Ex · ercitus,** -ūs, M.[ARC-],*trained body of men; army,* 1, 2, 5, etc.

**Ex · iguitās,** -ātis, F., *scantiness, shortness,* 24, 33.

**Ex · imius,** -a, -um [EM-], *taken out from; eminent, excellent, high,* 8.

**Ex · īstimō, 1,** *judge, value; judge, think, believe,* 2, 15, 17, 31; w. acc. and infin.

**Ex · pedītus,** -a, -um, adj. (P. of expediō) [PED-], *unencumbered, in light marching order,* 19.

**Ex · pellō, 3,** -pulī, -pulsum [PAL-, PEL-], *drive out, banish,* 4.

**Ex · perior, 4,** -pertus [1 PAR-, PER-], *try thoroughly; test, try,* 16.

**Ex · plōrātor,** -ōris, M. [PLV-(PLOV-)], *searcher out; scout, · spy,* 5, 11, 17. Cf. speculātor.

**Ex · plōrō, 1** [PLV- (PLOV-)], *search out; try to find out, reconnoitre,* 4.

**Ex · pūgnō, 1** [PAC-, PAG-, PVG-], *take by storm; take,* 9, 10, 12.

**Ex · spectō, 1** [SPEC-], *look out for greatly; wait for, await,* 9, 16, 20.

**Ex · struō, 3,** -strūxī, -strūctum [STRV-], *pile up thoroughly; erect, construct,* 30.

**Extrēmus,** -a, -um, adj., *furthest; most distant, extreme,* 5, 8, 25; *last,* 11, 27, 33.

**F.**

**Facile,** adv. [FAC-], *easily,* 1, 6, 17, 18, 19, 25.

**Facilis,** -e, adj. [FAC-], *able to be done; easy,* 27.

**Faciŏ, 3**, fēcī, factum ; pass. fĭō, fierī, factus [FAC-], *do, perform,* 3, 5, 6, etc. ; *make,* 1, 2, 6, etc. ; *cause, bring about,* 4, 11. See certus.

**Facultās**, -ātis, F. [FAC-], *power of doing; opportunity ;* pl. *resources, facilities,* 1.

**Fallō, 3**, fefellī, falsum, *cause to stumble ; deceive,* 10.

**Fastīgātus**, -a, -um, adj. (P. of fastīgō), *brought to a point; sloping,* 8. Cf. adclīvis, dēclīvis.

**Ferāx**, -ācis, adj. [1 FER-], *apt to bear ; fertile,* 4.

**Ferē**, adv. [2 FER-, FRE-], *nearly, almost,* 23, 25, 31.

**Ferō**, ferre, tulī, lātum [1 FER-], *bear, bring, carry,* 10, 26, 28 ; *bear, endure,* 1, w. acc. and infin. ; *rush* (in pass.), 24.

**Fertilitās**, -ātis, F. [1 FER-], *fruitfulness, fertility,* 4.

**Ferus**, -a, -um, adj., *wild, fierce, ferocious,* 4, 15.

**Fidēs**, fidē (rare), F.[1 FID-], *trust, confidence; protection,* 3, 13, 14, 15.

**Fīlius**, -ī, M., *son,* 13.

**Fīnis**, -is, M. [2 FID-], *dividing thing ; end, limit,* 6, 19 ; pl. *land, territory,* 2, 4, 5, etc.

**Fīnitimus**, -a, -um, adj. [2 FID-], *bordering upon; neighboring,* 2 ; pl. *neighbors,* 4, 16, 17, 28, 29, 31.

**Fĭō**, fierī, factus, *be made, become,* see **faciō**.

**Flūmen**, -inis, N., *that which flows ; river,* 5, 9, 10, etc.

**Fŏrs**, fŏrte, nom. and abl. only,

F. [1 FER-], *that which brings ; chance,* 21.

**Fŏrte**, adv., abl. of fŏrs, *by chance; perhaps,* 31.

**Fortis**, -e, adj. [2 FER-], *courageous, brave, stout-hearted,* 25, 33.

**Fort·iter**, adv. [2 FER-], *bravely, gallantly,* 11, 21, 26.

**Fŏrtūna**, -ae, F. [1 FER-], *fortune,* 16, 22, 31.

**Fossa**, -ae, F., *thing dug ; ditch,* 5, 8, 12, 32.

**Frāter**, -tris, M., *brother,* 3.

**Fremitus**, -ūs, M.,.*dull roar ; din, noise,* 24. Cf. strepitus.

**Frōns**, -ntis, F. [FVR-, FERV-], *brow ; front,* 8, 23, 25.

**Frūmentārius**, -a, -um, adj. [1 FVG-, FRVG-], *of grain,* w. res, *grain supply,* 2, 10.

**Frūmentum**, -ī, N. [1 FVG-, FRVG-], *thing eaten; corn, grain,* 3.

**Fuga**, -ae, F. [2 FVG-], *fleeing; flight, rout,* 11, 12, 23, 24, 26, 27.

**Fugiŏ, 3**, fūgī, — [2 FVG-], *flee, fly,* 11, 24.

**Fūmus**, -ī, M., *rushing thing; smoke,* 7.

**Funditor**, -ōris, M., *slinger,* 7, 10, 19, 24.

**Furor**, -ōris, M. [FVR-], *raging; blind passion, madness,* 3.

## G.

**Galba**, -ae, M., *king of the Suessiones,* 4, 13.

**Galea**, -ae, F. [2 CAL-, SCAL-], *covering; helmet,* 21.

**Gallia,** -ae, F., *Gaul,* 1, 2, 3, 4, 35.

**Gallus,** -ī, M., *a Gaul,* 1, 2, 4, 6, 12, 17, 24, 30.

**Gēns,** gentis, F., *what is begotten; race, tribe,* 28.

**Germānī,** -ōrum, M., *Germans,* 1, 3, 4.

**Gerō,** 3, gessī, gestum [GER-], *bear; carry on, go on with,* 9, 31, 35 ; pass., *be carried on, take place,* 2, 26 ; rès gestae, *operations, campaigns,* 35.

**Gladius,** -ī, M. [CEL-, CER-], *sword,* 23, 25.·

**Grātia,** -ae, F., *favor, popularity, influence,* 6.

**Gravis,** -e, adj., *heavy; severe, serious,* 25.

## H.

**Habeō,** 2 [HAB-], *grasp; have, possess,* 1, 3, 4, 8, 29 ; with reflex pronoun, *be,* 19.

**Hībernācula,** -ōrum, N. [HĪM-], *winter quarters,* 35.

**Hībernus,** -a, -um, adj. [HĪM-], *belonging to winter;* hīberna (castra), *winter quarters,* 1.

**Hī·o,** haec, hōc, demonstr. pron. [CA-, CI-], *this, this of mine,* 1, 2, 4, etc. ; *he, she, it,* 3, 4, 9, etc.

**Hiemō,** 1 [HĪM-], *pass the winter,* 1.

**Homō,** -inis, M. [HAM-], *man, person,* 1, 4, 6, 15, 27, etc.

**Honōs** (honor), -ōris, M., *honor, distinction,* 15.

**⁓stis,** -is, M., *one who hurts; my,* 5, 7, 8, 9, etc.

## I.

**Iaceō,** 2, -uī, — [IA- IAC-], *be thrown; lie,* 27.

**Iaciō,** 3, iēcī, iactum [IA-, IAC-], *hurl, throw,* 6, 32, 33 ; *throw up, construct,* 12.

**Iam,** adv., *at this* or *that time; now,* 19 ; neque iam, *and no longer,* 5, 20, 25, 33.

**Ibī,** adv. [2 I-], *in that place, there,* 4, 5, 8, etc.

**Iccius,** -ī, M., *Belgian of high rank,* 3, 6, 7.

**Ī·dem,** eadem, ídem, determ. pron. [2 I-; 3 DA-], *the very; same,* 3, 6, 7, 16, etc.

**Iden·t·idem,** adv. [2 I-], *very same; again and again,* 19.

**Ī·dōneus,** -a, -um, adj. [2 I-], *fit; suitable,* 8, 17.

**Īgnis,** -is, M. [AG-], *fire; camp-fire,* 7 ; *signal-fire, beacon,* 33.

**Ille,** -a, -ud, gen. illīus, demonstr. pron. [ANA-], *that; that one, the former,* 9, 33 ; *latter,* 19.

**Illyricum,** -ī, N., *coastland on eastern side of upper Adriatic,* 35.

**Im·pedīmentum (inp-),** -ī, N. [PED-], *thing entangling; hindrance,* 25 ; pl., *baggage,* 17, 24, 29 ; *baggage-train, pack-animals,* 17, 19, 24, 26. Cf. sarcina.

**Im·pediō (inp-),** 4 [PED-], *get the feet in, entangle; hinder, embarrass, make difficult,* 9, 10, 17, 20, 22, 23, 28.

**Im·pellō (inp-),** 3, -pulī, -pulsum [PAL-, PEL-, PVL-], *drive on; incite, influence,* 14.

**Im·perātor** (inp-), -ōris, M. [2 PAR-, POR-], *commander* (in chief), 25, 26.

**Im·perātum, -ī, N., *command*, 3,35.

**Im·perium** (inp-), -ī, N. [2 PAR-, POR-], *command, order*, 1, 20, 22 ; *chief command, authority*, 4, 23 ; *power, control*, 1, 3, 11.

**Im·perō** (inp-), 1 [2 PAR-, POR-], *put a command upon ; impose upon, command*, 3, 21, 28, 32, 35 ; *direct, dictate*, 11, 33 ; w. dat. and subjunctive w. ut.

**Im·petrō** (inp-), 1 [POT-], *accomplish ; obtain, succeed in obtaining a request*, 12 ; w. ut and subjunctive.

**Im·petus** (inp-), -ūs, M. [PET-], *onset, attack, charge*, 11, 19, 21, 24, 25 ; *fury, violence*, 6.

**Im·prō·vīsus** (inp-), -a, -um, adj. [VID-], *not foreseen ;* dē imprōvīsō, *unexpectedly, without notice*, 3.

**In,** prep. w. acc. and abl. [ANA-], *into, to*, 2, 3, 5 ; *in*, 5, 8, 29, etc. ; *in, within, on*, 1, 2, 8, etc. ; *upon, over*, 5, 29, 30 ; *among*, 25 ; *in the case of*, 32.

**In·cendō, 3,** -dī, -cēnsum, *put fire in ; set on fire*, 7.

**In·cĭdō, 3,** -cĭdī, — [CAD-], *fall into ; happen, occur*, 14. Cf. accĭdō, ēveniō.

**In·cīdō, 3,** -cīdī, -cīsum [2 SAC-, SEC-, SCĪD-, CĪD-], *cut into, notch*, 17.

**In·cipiō, 3,** -cēpī, -ceptum [CAP-], *take in hand ; begin*, 2 ; w. compl. infin.

**In·cĭtō,** 1 [CI-], *set in rapid motion ; urge on, hurry, hasten*, 26. Cf. impellō.

**In·colō, 3,** -uī, — *inhabit, live in*, 4 ; *live, dwell*, 3, 35.

**In·crē·dibilis,** -e, adj. [CRAT- ; 2 DA-], *not to be believed ; marvellous, incredible*, 19.

**In·crepitō, 1,** —, —, *make noise against ; upbraid, taunt, abuse*, 15, 30.

**In·ōūsō, 1** [CAV-], *make charges against, accuse, rebuke*, 15.

**Inde,** adv. [2 I-], *from that ; then, next*, 19.

**In·dĭgnitās,** -ātis, F., *unworthiness ; outrage, insult*, 14.

**In·dī·ligen·ter,** adv. [1 LEG-, LIG-], *carelessly, listlessly*, 33.

**In·dūcō, 3,** -xī, -ductum [DVC-], *lead into ; draw on, cover*, 33.

**Ind·uō, 3,** -uī, -ūtum, *put into ; put on*, 21.

**In·eō,** -īre, -īvī and -iī, -itum [1 I-], *go into ; enter upon, undertake*, 33 ; *begin*, 2, 35.

**In·ermis,** -e, adj. [AR-], *without armor ; unarmed*, 27.

**Īnferior,** -ius, adj. (compar. of īnferus ), *lower*, 25 ; *inferior*, 8.

**Īnfimus,** -a, -um, adj. (superl. of above), *lowest ; lowest part of, bottom*, 18.

**Īn·ferō,** -ferre, -tulī, illātum (inlatum) [1 FER-], *bring into ; make upon, wage*, 14, 29 ; *inspire in*, 25 ; *bring upon, cause, inflict*, 14, 32 ; *carry forward, advance*, 25, 26 ; *bring in, import*, 15 ; w. acc., or acc. and dat.

**ĭn·flectō, 3,** -flēxī, -flexum, *bend, bend down,* 17.

**In·gredior, 3,** -gressus [GRAD-], *go into, enter,* 4.

**In·imīcus, -a,** -um, adj. [AM-], *not friendly; hostile,* 31. Cf. hostis.

**In·īquitās,** -ātis, ꜰ. [IC-, AIC-], *unevenness, inequality,* 22.

**In·īquus,** -a, -um, adj. [IC-, AIC-], *not equal; uneven, unfavorable,* 10, 23, 27, 33.

**In·itium,** -ī, ɴ. [1 I-], *entering upon; beginning,* 9; w. partit. gen.

**In·iūria,** -ae, ꜰ. [IV-, IVG-], *thing done contrary to justice; wrong, injury, violence,* 28, 32, 33.

**In·nītor, 3,** -nīxus, *lean upon, prop one's self on,* 27.

**In·rīdeō (irr-), 2,** -rīsī, -rīsum, *laugh in ridicule; laugh at, mock,* 30.

**In·sequor, 3,** -secūtus [SEC-], *follow close upon; follow up, pursue,* 19, 23.

**In·sidiae,** -ārum, ꜰ. [SED-, SID-], *taking a position at; stratagem, trap, snare,* 11.

**In·signe,** -is, ɴ. [3 SAC-], *distinctive mark; sign, signal,* 20; *ornament, crest,* 21.

**In·sistō, 3,** -stitī, — [STA-], *set one's self on; take a stand on,* 27; w. dat.

**In·star,** indecl., ɴ., *image;* used as pred. adj., *like, in form of,* 17; w. gen.

**In·stō, 1,** -stitī, -statūrus [STA-], *stand upon; press forward,* 25.

**In·struō, 3,** -strūxī, -strūctum [STRV-], *build into; arrange,*

*draw up,* 8, 20, 22; *build, erect,* 30.

**Intel·legō (interl-), 3,** -lēxī, -lēctum [1 LEG-], *choose between; understand, be aware, know, find out,* 8, 10, 33; w. acc. and infin.; 14, w. indir. quest.

**Inter,** prep. w. acc. [ANA-], *in the midst; between,* 9, 17; *among,* 1, 4, 6, 15, 19, 24, 31.

**Inter·cēdō, 3,** -cessī, -cessum [CAD-], *go between; be between, move between,* 17.

**Inter·cipiō, 3,** -cēpī, -ceptum [CAP-], *take between; intercept,* 27.

**Inter·eā,** adv. [ANA-; 2 I-] *between these things; in the meantime, meanwhile.*

**Inter·ficiō, 3,** -fēcī, -fectum [FAC-], *make to be between, break in pieces; kill, put to death,* 10, 11, 23, 25, 31. Cf. concīdō, occīdō.

**Inter·iciō, 3,** -iēcī, -iectum [IA-, IAC-], *hurl between; place or plant among,* 17; pass., *intervene,* 22.

**Inter·im,** adv. [ANA-; 2 I-], *in the meantime, meanwhile,* 9, 12, 19, 26.

**Interior,** -ius, adj., compar. of obsolete interus [ANA-], *inner, interior of,* 2.

**Inter·mittō, 3,** -mīsī, -missum [MIT-], *make go apart; discontinue, cease,* 25.

**Inter·neciō,** -ōnis, ꜰ. [1 NEC-, NOC-], *complete destruction, annihilation,* 28.

**Inter·scindō, 3,** -scidī, -scissum

[2 SAC-, SEC-, SCĪD-], *separate by splitting ; cut down, hew away, demolish,* 9.

**Inter·sum,** -esse, -fuī [ES-], *be between ; be the concern of, concern,* 5 ; w. gen. of price.

**Inter·vāllum,** -ī, N. [1 VEL-, VAL-], *space between stakes of a palisade ; distance, interval,* 23. Cf. spatium.

**In·texō,** 3, -uī, -xtum [TEC-, TAX-], *weave in ; plait,* 33.

**Intrā,** prep. w. acc. [ANA-], *on the inside ; within,* 4, 18, 19.

**Intrō,** 1 [ANA-], *enter, penetrate,* 17.

**Intrō·dūcō,** 3, -xī, -ductum [DVC-], *lead in, bring in,* 5, 10.

**Intrō·mittō,** 3, -mīsī, -missum [MIT-], *cause to go within ; let in, admit,* 33.

**Intr·ōrsus,** adv. [VERT-], *towards the inside ; into the interior, within,* 18.

**In·ūsitātus,** -a, -um, adj. [1 AV-], *unusual, strange,* 31.

**In·ūtilis,** -e, adj. [1 AV-], *useless ; unserviceable, incapable,* 16 ; w. ad and acc.

**In·veniō,** 4, -vēnī, -ventum [BA-, VA-, VEN-], *come upon ; find, learn,* 16 ; w. acc. and infin. Cf. cōgnōscō.

**In·veterāscō,** 3, -āvī, — [VET-], *become of long standing ; gain a permanent foothold,* 1.

**In·videō,** 2, -vīdī, -vīsum [VID-], *look towards ; be jealous of, envy,* 31.

**I·pse,** -a, -um (gen. ipsīus), intensive pron. [2 I- ; 3 SA-], *per-*

*son* or *thing mentioned ; self,* 3, 4, 5, etc.; *sometimes conveniently rendered he, they (the latter),* 2, 20, 29.

**Is,** ea, id, determ. pron. [2 I-], *person* or *thing mentioned ; he, that, this,* 1, 2, 3, etc. ; akin to talis, foll. by subj. clause, 9, 16.

**Ita,** adv. [2 I-], *in the way stated ; so, thus,* 11, 33 ; w. ut, *in the way that, just as, as,* 1.

**Ītalia,** -ae, F., *Italy,* 29, 35.

**Ita·que,** conj. [2 I- ; CA-, CI-], *and so ; therefore,* 7, 22.

**Item,** adv. [2 I-], *even so ; so, likewise,* 1, 8, 13, 21, 23, 26.

**Iter,** itineris, N. [1 I-], *going ; march, route, line of march, road,* 6, 11, 12, 16, 17, 29.

**Iubeō,** 2, iūssī, iūssum [IV-, IVG-], *order, command, bid,* 5, 11. 25, 28, 33, 35 ; w. acc. and infin.

**Iū·dicō,** 1 [IV-, IVG-; DIC-], *declare what is law ; judge, suppose, think,* 27.

**Iugum,** -ī, N. [IV-, IVG-], *joining ; ridge, chain of hills,* 24.

**Iūs,** iūris, N. [IV-, IVG-], *thing binding ; constitution, law,* 3.

**Iūstitia,** -ae, F. [IV- IVG-], *uprightness, justice, fairness,* 4.

**Iuvō,** 1, iūvī, iūtum [DIV-, DI-, DIAV-], *delight ; help, assist,* 3.

**Iūxtā,** adv. [IV-, IVG-], *closely joined ; close by, near at hand,* 26.

### L.

**L.,** *prænomen Lucius,* 11.

**Labiēnus,** -ī, M., *Titus Labienus,*

*most eminent of Cæsar's lieutenants*, 1, 11, 26.

**Lapis**, -idis, M., *stone*, 6.

**Lassitūdō**, -inis, F. [LAG-], *faintness, exhaustion*, 23.

**Lateō**, 2, -uī, —, *lie hidden; be concealed*, 19.

**Lātitūdō**, ·inis, F. [STER-, STRA-, STLA-], *breadth; width, expanse, extent*, 7, 8, 12, 29; *lateral direction*, 17.

**Lātus**, -a, -um, adj. [STER-, STRA-, STLA-], *extended; broad, wide*, 4, 27.

**Latus**, -eris, N. [PLAT-], *thing extending; side, flank*, 5, 8, 23, 25.

**Laxō, 1** [LAG], *loose; change to open order, widen*, 25.

**Lēgātiō**, -ōnis, F. [3 LEG-], *embassy, legation*, 35.

**Lēgātus**, -ī, M. [3 LEG-], *envoy*, 6, 12, 15, 28, 31, 35; *lieutenant*, 2, 5, 9, 11, 20.

**Legiō**, -ōnis, F. [1 LEG-], *levying; largest military division, consisting of 10 cohorts; legion*, 2, 8, 17, etc.

**Legiōnārius**, -a, -um, adj. [1 LEG-], *belonging to a legion; legionary*, 27.

**Lēn·iter**, adv. [1 I-], *gently, moderately*, 8, 29.

**Levis**, -e, adj. [2 LEG-], *lightly moving; light*, 10, 24.

**Levitās**, -ātis, F. [2 LEG-], *lightness; inconstancy, fickleness*, 1.

**Lēx**, lēgis, F. [3 LEG-], *thing read; written law, law*, 3. Cf. iūs.

**Līberāl·iter**, adv. [LIB-; 1 I-], *generously, graciously*, 5.

**Līberī**, -erōrum, M. [LIB-], *those who do as they desire, free persons; children (of free parents)*, 5.

**Littera**, -ae, F. [LI-], *written character;* pl., *letter, letters; despatch, despatches*, 1, 2, 35.

**Locus**, -ī, M., *that placed or situated; place, point, position, situation*, 2, 4, 5, etc.; *state, condition*, 26; pl., **loca**, -ōrum, N., *region, section, tract*, 4, 19.

**Longē**, adv. [2 LEG-], *in length; far, at a distance*, 4, 5, 19, 20, 21.

**Longus**, -a, -um, adj. [2 LEG-], *long, lengthy*, 21.

**Loquor**, 3, locūtus, *speak, talk*, 31.

**Lūx**, lūcis, F., *that which shines; light, dawn, daylight*, 11.

### M.

**Māchinātiō**, -ōnis, F., *contrivance, engine, machine*, 30, 31.

**Magis**, adv. [MAC-, MAG-], *in a higher degree; more*, 22, 32.

**Magistrātus**, -ūs, M. [MAC-, MAG-], *magistracy, ruler*, 3.

**Māgnitūdō**, -inis, F. [MAC-, MAG-], *greatness, size, height*, 12, 27, 30.

**Māgnus**, -a, -um, adj. [MAC-, MAG-], *increased; great*, 4, 5, 6, etc.

**Māior**, -ius, adj., compar. of above, *greater;* māior nātū, *elder*, 13, 28.

**Male·ficium**, -ī, N. [MAL-; FAC-], *evil-doing; outrage, hostile act*, 28. Cf. iniūria, indīgnitās.

**Man·dŏ, 1** [1 MA-, MAN- ; 2 DA-], *put into one's hands ; give in charge, enjoin, order,* 5 ; *entrust, consign,* 24 ; w. acc. and dat.

**Mani·pulus,-ī, M.** [1 MA-, MAN- ; PLE-, PLV-], *thing filling the hand ; (subdivision of a cohort), company, maniple,* 25.

**Mān·suētūdŏ, -inis, F.** [1 MA-, MAN- ; SOVO-, SVO-], *tameness ; gentleness, kindness,* 14, 31. Cf. clēmentia.

**Manus, -ūs, F.** [1 MA-, MAN-], *measuring thing ; hand,* 13, 19, 30 ; *band, force,* 2, 5.

**Maritimus (-umus), -a, -um, adj.,** *of the sea ; on the coast, maritime,* 34.

**Mātūrŏ, 1,** *make ripe ; hasten, make haste,* 5. Cf. contendŏ.

**Māximē, adv.,** superl. of magis, q. v. ; *most, very,* 4.

**Medius, -a, -um, adj.,** *in the middle ; middle of,* 7.

**Memoria, -ae, F.** [1 SMAR-, MAR-], *faculty of remembering ; recollection, memory,* 4, 21.

**Menapiī, -ōrum, M.,** *Gallic tribe between the Meuse and Scheld,* 4.

**Mercātor, -ōris, M.** [2 SMAR-, MER-], *trader,* 15.

**Meritum, -ī, N.** [2 SMAR-, MER-], *thing deserved ; deserts, merit,* 32.

**Mīles, -itis, M.** [MĪL-], *one of the thousand ; soldier,* 11, 20, 21, etc.

**Mīlitāris, -e, adj.** [MĪL-], *of soldiers ; pertaining to war, military,* 4, 22.

**Mīlle,** pl. mīlia or mīllia, num.

adj. [MĪL-], *large number associated ; thousand,* 4, 6, 7, etc.

**Minimē, adv.,** superl. of minus, *least,* 33.

**Minor, -us, adj.** [2 MAN-, MI-], *smaller ;* minus, N., as adv., *less,* 1, 7, 20 ; *not* (=nōn), 9.

**Miser, -era, -erum, adj.** [MIS-], *wretched, miserable,* 28.

**Miserī·cordia, -ae, F.** [MIS-], *heart-pity ; pity, compassion,* 28.

**Mittŏ, 3,** mīsī, mīssum [MIT-], *let go ; send, despatch,* 2, 3, 5, etc.

**Mŏbilitās, -ātis, F.** [1 MV-, MOV-], *ability to be moved, agility ; fickleness, inconstancy,* 1. Opp. to stabilitās. Cf. levitās.

**Modo, adv.** [2 MA-, MAD-], *in a measure ; only, merely,* 17, 21.

**Modus, -ī, M.** [2 MA-, MAD-], *measuring thing ; manner, fashion,* 31.

**Moenia, -ium, N.** [2 MV-], *things that ward off ; walls, city walls,* 6, 31.

**Molestē, adv.** [1 MAC-, MAG-], *in a troublesome manner ;* molestē ferre, *be annoyed* or *vexed,* 1 ; w. acc. and infin.

**Moneŏ, 2** [1 MAN-, MEN-], *cause to think ; direct,* 26 ; w. acc., foll. by clause w. ut.

**Mora, -ae, F.** [1 SMAR-, MAR-], *stopping, delay,* 15.

**Morinī, -ōrum, M.,** *tribe of Belgæ on Channel, near Calais,* 4.

**Moror, 1** [1 SMAR-, MAR-], *linger, tarry, delay,* 7, 10, 11.

**Mōs, mōris, M.** [1 MA-, MAN-],

*will; custom, manner,* 13, 15.
Cf. cōnsuētūdō.

**Moveō, 2,** mōvī, mōtum [1 MV-, MOV-], *set in motion; move,* 2, 31.

**Mulier, -eris, F.** [MAL-], *woman, female,* 13, 16, 28.

**Multitūdō, -inis, F.,** *large number, body,* 4, 5, 6, etc. ; *quantity, number,* 10, 32.

**Multus, -a, -um, adj.,** *much,* pl. *many,* 11, 25, 29.

**Mūnīmentum, -ī, N.** [2 MV-], *means of defence; fortification, defence,* 17.

**Mūniō, 4** [2 MV-], *wall; fortify, erect defences about, protect, make,* (castra), 5, 12, 19, 20, 29.

**Mūnītiō, -ōnis, F.** [2 MV-], *fortifying; fortification, works,* 33.

**Mūrus, -ī, M.** [2 MV-], *encircling thing; wall, city wall,* 6, 12, 13, 17, 29, 30, 32. Cf. moenia.

### N.

**Nam,** co-ord. conj. [GNA-], *for,* 6, 14, 16, 19, 23, 30 ; as enclitic, quisnam, *really, pray,* 30. Cf. the postpositive enim.

**Nāscor, 3,** nātus [GEN-, GNA-], *be born; begin, arise,* 18.

**Nātiō, -ōnis, F.** [GEN-, GNA-], *birth; race, people,* 35. Cf. populus, gēns.

**Nātūra, -ae, F.** [GEN-, GNA-], *birth; nature, character,* 8, 15, 18, 22, 29.

**(Nātus, -ūs),** only abl. sing., M. [GEN-, GNA-], *birth,* 13, 28.

**Nāvō, 1** [GNA-, GNO-], *perform with knowledge and zeal; do one's best, exert one's self,* 25.

**Nē,** adv. and conj. [NA-], *no;* adv., *not,* 3, 17 ; conj., *that not, lest* (after expressions involving fear), 1, 5, 8, etc.

**Necessārius, -a, -um, adj.** [2 NEC-], *unavoidable; pressing, urgent,* 21.

**Necessitās, -ātis, F.** [2 NEC-], *unavoidableness; necessity, compulsion,* 11 ; *urgency,* 22.

**Neg·ōtium, -ī, N.,** [1 AV-], *not leisure; business, task,* 2 ; *trouble, difficulty,* 17.

**Nē·mō, —,** dat. nēminī, abl. wanting, M. and F. [HAM-], *no man; nobody, no one,* 33.

**Ne·que** or **nec,** adv. [NA-; CA-, CI-], *and not, and so not,* 3, 5, 10, etc. ; neque . . . neque, *neither . . . nor,* 11, 12, 15, 25.

**Nē·quī·quam,** adv. [CA-, CI-], *not in any way; to no purpose, in vain,* 27.

**Nervii, -ōrum, M.,** *most warlike tribe of the Belgæ,* 4, 15, 16, etc.

**Neuter, -tra, -trum,** gen. -trīus, adj. [CA-, CI-], *neither (of two),* 9.

**Nē·ve** or **neu,** conj. [NA-], *and not; and that not,* 21.

**Nihil,** indecl., N. [NA-], *nothing,* 15, 26, 28 ; as adv., *not at all,* 17, 20.

**Ni·si,** conj. [NA-; SOVO-, SVO-], *if not, unless, except,* 6, 20, 32.

**Nōbilitās, -ātis, F.** [GNA-, GNO-], *being known; high birth,* 6.

**Noctū**, adv. [1 NEC-, NOC-], *by night*, 33.

**Nōlō**, nōlle, nōluī, —, [VOL-], *not wish; be unwilling*, 1.

**Nōmen**, -inis, N. [GNA-, GNO-], *means of knowing; name*, 4, 6, 28.

**Nōminātim**, adv. [GNA-, GNO-]. *by name, expressly*, 25.

**Nōminō**, 1 [GNA-, GNO-], *name, mention*, 18.

**Nōn**, adv. [NA-; 2 I-], *not one; not*, 2, 6, 8, etc.

**Nōn·dum**, adv. [NA-; ĐIV-], *not yet*, 11.

**Nōn·nūllus**, -a, -um, adj. [2 I-], *not none; some*, 1, 25.

**Nōnūs**, -a, -um, adj., *ninth*, 23.

**Nōs**, nostrum, pl. of ego, pron. [NV-], *we*, 9.

**Noster**, -stra, -strum, poss. pron. [NV-], *our, ours*, 1, 4, 8, etc.

**Novem**, num. adj., indecl., *nine*, 4.

**Noviodūnum**, -ī, N., *chief town of Suessiones*, 12.

**Novus**, -a, -um, adj. [NV-], *new, fresh*, 1, 2 ; *strange, novel*, 31 ; superl., *last, in the rear*, 11, 25, 26.

**Nox**, -ctis, F. [1 NEC-, NOC-], *night*, 6, 7, 12, 17.

**Nūdō**, 1, *make bare; bare, strip*, 6 ; *leave unguarded*, 23.

**N·ūllus**, -a, -um, adj. [2 I-], *not any; none, no*, 11, 15, 32 ; as dat. of nēmō, *no one*, 6, 35.

**Numerus**, -ī, M., *distributed thing; number, amount, numbers*, 4, 10, 17, 33.

**Numida**, -ae, M., *Numidian*, 7, 10, 24.

**Nun·c**, adv. [NV-; CA-, CI-], *now, at the present time*, 4.

**Nūntiō**, 1 [NV-], *announce, report*, 2, 26, 28, 29, 32.

**Nūntius**, -ī, M. [NV-], *person or thing newly come; messenger*, 7 ; *message, news*, 2, 6 ; w. acc. and infin.

## O.

**Ob**, prep. w. acc. [APA-], *towards; on account of*, 35.

**Ob·dūcō, 3**, -xī, -ductum [DVC-], *lead towards; extend, construct*, 8.

**Ob·itus** (-ūs), M. [1 I-], *going to ; destruction*, 29. Cf. interneciō.

**Ob·sēs**, -idis, M. and F. [SED-], *one staying in a place; hostage*, 1, 3, 5, 13, 15, 35.

**Ob·tineō, 2**, -uī, -tentum [1 TA-, TEN-], *lay hold of ; have possession of, hold*, 4.

**Ob·veniō, 4**, -vēnī, -ventum [BA-, VA-, VEN-], *come in the way of ; come against, meet*, 23 ; w. dat.

**Oc·cāsus** (obc-), -ūs, M. [CAD-], *going down ; setting*, 11.

**Oc·cīdō** (obc-), **3**, -cīdī, -cīsum [2 SAC-, SCĪD-, CĪD-], *strike against; kill, slay*, 10, 25, 33.

**Oc·cultus** (obc-), -a, -um, adj. (P. of occulō) [2 CAL-], *covered over ; hidden, secret*, 18.

**Oc·cupō** (obc-), **1** [CAP-], *take hold of ; cover, occupy*, 8 ; *take possession of, hold*, 1 ; pass., *be engaged, occupy one's self*, 19.

**Oc·currō** (obc-), **3**, -currī, -cursum [CEL-, CER-], *run towards ;*

*fall in with, meet; come against,*
21, 24, 27. Cf. obveniō.

**Ōceanus,** -ī, M., *ocean, Atlantic,*
34.

**Octāvus,** -a, -um, adj., *eighth,* 23.

**Octŏ,** num. adj., indecl., *eight,*
6, 7.

**Of·ferŏ** (obf-), -ferre, obtulī,
oblātum [1 FER-], *bring
towards; offer, bear, carry,* 21.

**O·mittŏ, 3,** -mīsī, -missum
[MIT-], *let go; neglect, leave
untried,* 17.

**Omnis,** -e, adj. [AP-, OP-], *every,
all, entire,* 1, 2, 3, etc.

**Onus,** -eris, N. [AN-], *burden;
bulk, weight,* 30.

**Opera,** -ae, F. [AP-, OP-], *working; work, service,* 25.

**Opīniŏ,** -ōnis, F. [AP-, OP-],
*thinking; impression, idea, ex-
pectation,* 3, 35; *reputation,* 8, 24.

**O·portet, 2,** -uit, —, impers.
[2 PAR-, POR-], *is necessary;
must, ought,* 20; w. pass. infin.
or acc. and infin.

**Op·pidānus** (obp-), -a, -um,
adj. [PED-], *of a town;* as
noun, M., *townsman, inhabitant
of a town* (*other than Rome*), 7,
33.

**Op·pidum** (obp-), -ī, N. [PED-],
*on the ground; town,* 3, 4, 6,
etc. Cf. urbs; vīcus.

**Op·portūnus** (obp-), -a, -um,
adj. [1 PAR-, PER-], *of what
is opposite the harbor; suitable,
convenient,* 8. Cf. idōneus.

**Op·pūgnātiŏ** (obp-), -ōnis, F.
[PAC-, PVG-], *act of assault-
ing; mode of attack, assault,* 6.

**Op·pūgnŏ, 1** [PAC-, PVG-],
*fight against; attack, storm,* 6;
*carry by assault,* 12.

**(Ops),** opis, F. (no nom. or dat.
sing.) [AP-, OP-], *obtaining
thing; help, aid,* 31; pl., *re
sources,* 14.

**Optimus,** -a, -um, adj. used as
superl. of bonus [AP-, OP-]
*best,* 10.

**Opus, -eris,** N. [AP-, OP-], *obtaining thing; work, siege-work,*
12, 19, 20, 21; quantō opere,
*how greatly,* māgnō opere, *very
much,* 5.

**Opus,** indecl. N. (really same word
as above) [AP-, OP-], w. est, *is
necessary, is need,* 8, 22.

**Ōrātiŏ,** -ōnis, F., *speaking; address, speech, words,* 5, 21.

**Ōrdŏ,** -inis, M. [OL-, OR-], *weav-
ing; succession, order,* 11, 19,.
22; *rank, line,* 11, 19.

**Orior, 4,** ortus [OL-, OR-], *bestir
one's self; arise, be raised,* 24;
*be descended from,* 4.

**Osismī,** -ōrum, M., *people of Gaul*
(*in Brittany*), 34.

## P.

**P.,** abbrev. *of Publius,* 25, 34.

**Pābulum,** -ī, N. [PA-], *thing affect-
ing feeding; fodder, forage,* 2.

**Pācŏ, 1** [PAC-], *bring to peace;
subdue,* 1, 35.

**Paemānī,** -ōrum, M. *German tribe
of the Belgæ,* 4.

**Paene,** adv., *nearly, almost,* 19,
24.

**Palūs,** -ūdis, F., *thing having wet clay; marsh, swamp, morass,* 9, 16, 28.

**Pandō, 3,** -dī, passum [2 PAT-, PAD-], *cause to go; spread out, extend,* 13.

**Pār,** paris, adj. [1 PAR-, PER-], *equal,* 18.

**Parātus,** -a, -um, adj. (P. of parō) [2 PAR-, POR-], *brought; made ready, ready, prepared,* 3, 9, 21; w. infin. or expression of purpose.

**Pars,** partis, F. [2 PAR-, POR-], *that cut; part, portion,* 1, 4, 9, etc.; *quarter, direction,* 21, 24, 29; *point, side,* 5, 8, 22.

**Partim,** adv. (acc. of Pars) [2 PAR-, POR-], *by a dividing; partly,* 1, 33.

**Parvulus,** -a, -um, dim. adj. [PAV-], *very small; slight, unimportant,* 30.

**Passus,** -ūs, M. [1 PAT-], *going; double pace, step, pace,* 8, 18; mīlia passuum, *mile* (= 5000 feet), 6, 7, 11, 13, 16.

**Pate·faciō, 3,** -fēcī, -factum [2 PAT-; FAC-], *make open; open, throw open,* 32.

**Pateō, 2,** -uī, — [2 PAT-], *stand open; be open, spread out, extend,* 7, 8.

**Pater,** -tris, M. [PA-], *accomplisher of protecting* or *nourishing; father,* 4.

**Patior, 3,** passus, *suffer, endure,* 31; *suffer, allow,* 15.

**Patrius,** -a, -um, adj. [PA-], *of a father; of one's ancestors, ancestral,* 15.

**Paucus,** -a, -um, adj. [PAV-], *made to cease;* pl. only, *few,* 18; as substantive, *a few, small number,* 12.

**Paulātim,** adv. [PAV-], *by little and little; gradually, gently,* 8, 26.

**Paulis·per,** adv. [PAV-; 1 PAR-], *for a short time,* 7.

**Paulō,** adv. (abl. N. of paulus) [PAV-], *by a little; a little,* 20.

**Paululum,** dim. adv. [PAV-], *very little; very slightly,* 8.

**Paulum,** adv. (acc. N. of paulus) [PAV-], *a little,* 25.

**Pāx,** pācis, F. [PAC-], *binding thing; peace,* 6, 13, 15, 29, 31, 32.

**Pedēs,** -itis, M. [PED-], *one that goes on foot; foot-soldier,* 24.

**Pedester,** -tris, -tre, adj. [PED-], *of infantry, infantry,* 17.

**Pedius,** -ī, M., *Quintus Pedius,* Cæsar's nephew, and lieutenant under him, 2, 11.

**Pellis,** -is, F. [PLE-], *hide, skin,* 33.

**Pellō, 3,** pepulī, pulsum [PAL-, PEL-], *cause to move; drive, dislodge,* 24; *rout, defeat,* 17, 19, 24.

**Per,** prep. w. acc. [1 PAR-, PER-], *through; by, by means of,* 11, 20, 31; *on account of,* 16; *through, by way of,* 16; *over,* 10.

**Per·ferō,** -ferre, -tulī, -lātum [1 FER-], *carry through; bear, endure,* 14; *bear, spread among,* 35.

**Perīclitor, 1** [1 PAR-, PER-], *test; prove, make trial,* 8.

**Perīculum,** -ī, N. [1 PAR-, PER-],

*means of trying, trial; danger, peril*, 5, 11, 26.

**Per · mittō, 3**, -mīsī, -mīssum [MIT-], *let through; yield, give up*, 3, 31; w. acc. and dat.

**Per · moveō, 2**, -mōvī, -mōtum [1 MV-, MOV-], *stir up thoroughly; disturb, alarm*, 12, 24.

**Per · spiciō, 3**, -spēxī, -spectum [SPEC-], *see through*, 17, 18; *perceive clearly, find out, ascertain*, 11, 17, 32.

**Per · suādeō, 2**, -sī, -sum, *thoroughly advise; prevail upon, persuade*, 10, 16; w. dat. and subjunctive w. ut.

**Per · terreō, 2** [TER-], *thoroughly frighten; demoralize, render panic-stricken*, 24, 27. Cf. perturbō.

**Per · tineō, 2**, -uī, — [1 TA-, TEN-], *thoroughly hold; extend to*, 19.

**Per · turbō, 1** [TVR-], *throw into utter confusion; disconcert, alarm*, 11, 21. Cf. permoveō.

**Per · veniō, 4**, -vēnī, -ventum [BA-, VA-, VEN-], *come quite to; reach, arrive at*, 2, 11, 15, 17.

**Pēs**, pedis, м. [PED-], *going thing; foot*, 5, 18, 29, 30.

**Petō, 3**, -īvī and -iī, -ītum [PET-], *fall upon; seek*, 20, 24; *aim at, make for*, 11, 23; *seek, make request, ask*, 12, 14, w. ut and subjunct.; *ask, beg*, 13, 31, w. acc.

**Pīlum**, -ī, N. [PIS-], *crushing thing; heavy javelin*, 23, 27.

**Plānitiēs** (-ēī), F. [PLAT-], *flatness; level stretch of country, plain*, 8.

**Plērum · que**, adv. (acc. N. of plērusque), *for the most part, generally*, 30.

**Plērus · que**, -raque, -rumque, adj. [PLE-; CA-, CI-], *larger part of; most of*, 4.

**Plūrimus**, -a, -um, adj. (used as superl. of multus) [PLE-, PLO-, PLV-], *most;* acc. N. as adv., *most*, 4.

**Pol · liceor, 2** [LIC-, LIQV-], *offer very much; offer, promise*, 4, 35.

**Pondus**, -eris, N., *weighing thing; weight, bulk*, 29. Cf. onus.

**Pōnō** [for portsinō], **3**, posuī, positum [1 SA-, SI-], *let down; place, establish, pitch*, 5, 7, 8, 13; *place, base on*, 11.

**Pōns**, pontis, м. [1 PAT-], *means of going; bridge*, 5, 9, 10.

**Populor, 1** [SCAL-, SPOL-], *pour out people; lay waste, ravage, raid*, 5, 9. Cf. dēpopulor, vāstō.

**Populus**, -ī, м. [PLE-, PLO-], *the many; people, nation*, 1, 3, 13, etc. Cf. gēns.

**Por · rēctus**, -a, -um, adj. (P. of porrigō) [REG-, RIG-], *stretched out, stretched forward*, 19.

**Porta**, -ae, F. [1 PAR-, POR-], *thing passed through; gate*, 6, 24, 32, 33.

**Portō, 1** [1 PAR-, POR-], *bear along, carry, convey*, 5, 29.

**Poscō, 3**, poposcī, — [PREC-], *ask for urgently; demand, request*, 15. Cf. petō.

**Pos · sideō, 2**, -sēdī, -sessum [SED-], *have and hold, possess*, 4.

**Pos · sum**, posse, potuī [POT-],

*be able, can*, 1, 3, 4, etc.; *amount to, be influential* or *powerful*, 4, 8.

**Post**, prep. w. acc. [POS-], *behind; after*, 14, 29; *behind*, 5, 9, 19.

**Post·eā**, adv. [POS-; 2 I-], *after this; afterwards*, 17, 30, 32.

**Post·quam**, conj. [POS-; CA-], *after that; after, as soon as, when*, 5.

**Postrēmō**, *at last, finally*.

**Postrī·diē**, adv. (contr. from posterō diē) [POS-; DIV-, DI-], *on the day after*, 12, 33; w. gen.

**Postulō, 1** [PREC-], *ask, demand, require*, 4, 22, 33. Cf. poscō.

**Potēns**, -entis, adj. [POT-], *able, mighty, powerful*, 1, 4.

**Potestās**, -ātis, f. [POT-], *ability; power, control*, 3, 31, 34; *power, ability*, 6.

**Potior**, **4** [POT-], *become master of; get control of, gain*, 7, 24, 26; w. abl.

**Potius**, adv. (compar.) [POT-], *rather, preferably*, 10; foll. by quam.

**Prae**, prep. w. abl. [PRO-, PRI-, PRAE-], *before; in comparison with*, 30.

**Prae·acūtus**, -a, -um, adj. [1 AC-], *sharpened in front; pointed, sharpened at the point*, 29.

**Prae·beō** [for praehibeō], **2** [HAB-], *hold forth; furnish, afford*, 17.

**Prae·ceps**, -ipitis, adj. [CAP-], *head foremost; headlong, in haste*, 24.

**Prae·dor** [for praehedor], **1**, *make booty; plunder, raid*, 17, 24.

**Prae·ferō**, -ferre, -tulī, -lātum [1 FER-], *bear before; place before, thrust forward, outdo*, 27; w. acc. and dat.

**Prae·ficiō**, **3**, -fēcī, -fectum [FAC-], *place over; put at the head of, place in command of*, 11; w. acc. and dat.

**Prae·mittō**, **3**, -mīsī, -missum [MIT-], *send before; send in advance*, 11, 17, 19.

**Prae·scrībō**, **3**, -psī, -ptum [SCARP-, SCALP-], *write before; dictate, prescribe, direct*, 20; w. dat. and indir. question.

**Prae·sertim**, adv. [1 SER-, SVAR-], *by an arranging before; especially, particularly*, 30.

**Prae·sidium**, -ī, n. [SED-], *sitting before; guard, defence, support*, 5, 19, 26, 29, 33; *protection, safety*, 11.

**Prae·stō**, **1**, -stitī, — [STA-], *stand before; excel*, 15; *put forth, exhibit*, 27; *be preferable, be better* (impers.), 31.

**Prae·sum**, -esse, -fuī [ES-], *be before; be in charge of, command*, 6, 9; w. dat.

**Praeter·eā**, *in addition*.

**Premō**, **3**, pressī, pressum, *press; push closely, press hard*, 24.

**Prīmi·pīlus**, -ī, m. [PRO-, PRI-; PIS-], *first centurion of the triarii*, 25.

**Prīmō**, adv. [PRO-], *at first*, 8.

**Prīmum**, adv. (acc. n. of prīmus) [PRO-, PRI-], *first thing; first, in the first place*, 1, 10, 30; cum prīmum, *as soon as*, 2.

**Prīmus**, -a, -um, adj. [PRO-,

PRI-], *first, foremost,* 10, 11, 17, etc. ; as noun, M., *chief, leading man,* 3, 13.

**Prīn·ceps,** -ipis, adj. [PRO-, PRI- ; CAP-], *taking first place ;* as noun, *leader, chief,* 5, 14. Cf. prīmus.

**Prior,** -ius, gen. -ōris, adj. [PRO-, PRI-], *former ; those preceding, men in front,* 11. Opp. novissimī.

**Prīs·tinus,** -a, -um, adj. [PRO-, PRI- ; 1 TA-, TEN-] *former ; former, old time,* 21.

**Prius,** adv. (acc. N. of prior) [PRO-, PRI-], *earlier, sooner,* 32 ; foll. by quam.

**Prius·quam,** adv., conj. (= prius quam) [PRO-, PRI- ; CA-], *sooner than, before,* 12 ; w. subj. Cf. prius quam, 32.

**Prō,** prep. w. abl. [PRO-, PRI-], *before ; in front of, before,* 8 ; *in behalf of,* 14 ; *in proportion to, to the best of one's ability,* 25 ; *in accordance with, agreeably to,* 31.

**Prō·cēdō,** 3, -cessī, -cessum [CAD-], *go forward ; advance, proceed,* 20, 25.

**Pro·cul,** adv. [CEL-], *driven forward ; at a distance, afar off,* 30.

**Prō·cumbō,** 3, -cubuī, -cubitum, *bend forwards ; fall forward, sink to the ground,* 27.

**Proelior,** 1, *fight, contend,* 23. Cf. dīmicō, congredior.

**Proelium,** -ī, N., *fighting, fight,* 23, 25, 26, 27 ; *skirmish, engagement, battle,* 8, 9, 20, 21, 28, 30.

**Pro·fectiō,** -ōnis, F. [FAC-], *going away ; setting out, departure,* 11.

**Pro·ficīscor,** 3, -fectus [FAC-], *begin to go forward ; set out, go, march,* 2, 21, 25, 35.

**Prō·flīgō,** 1 [FLAG-, FLIG-], *strike to the ground ; rout, defeat,* 23. Cf. pellō, cōniciō.

**Pro·fugiō,** 3, -fūgī, — [2 FVG-], *flee before ; flee for refuge, escape,* 14.

**Prō·gnātus,** -a, -um, adj. [GEN-, GN-, GNA-], *born, descended, sprung from,* 29.

**Prō·gredior,** 3, -gressus [GRAD-], *go forward ; advance, proceed,* 10, 23. Cf. prōcēdō.

**Pro·hibeō,** 2 [HAB-], *hold before ; hinder, prevent,* 4, w. acc. and infin. ; *keep from, cut off,* 9, 28, w. acc. and abl.

**Prō·iciō,** 3, -iēcī, -iectum [IA-, IAC-], *cast forward ; give up, abandon, renounce,* 15.

**Prō·moveō,** 2, -mōvī, -mōtum [1 MV-, MOV-], *move forward, advance,* 31.

**Prope,** adv. [PARC-, PLEC-], *near ; nearly, almost,* 28, 32.

**Pro·perō,** 1 [2 PAR-, POR-], *hasten, make haste,* 11, 35.

**Propinquitās,** -ātis, F. [PARC-, PLEC-], *nearness, proximity,* 20 ; *family connection, kinship,* 4. Cf. adfīnitās.

**Propinquus,**-a, -um, adj. [PARC-, PLEC-], *being near ; near, close, adjacent,* 35, w. dat.

**Prō·pōnō,** 3, -posuī, -positum [1 SA-, SI-], *place before ; put forth, expose to view, display,* 20.

**Prop·ter,** prep. w. acc. [PARC-,

PLEC-], *near; on account of,* 4, 8, 12, 16, 20.

Propter·eā, adv. [PARC-, PLEC-], *on account of that; foll.* by quod, *for the reason (that), because,* 4; foll. by indic.

Prō·pūgnō, 1 [PAC-, PAG-, PVG-], *fight before; fight in defence, make defensive sallies,* 7.

Prō·sequor, 3, -secūtus [SEC-], *follow onward; pursue, follow after,* 11 ; *follow, address,* 5.

Prō·spectus, -ūs, M. [SPEC-], *forward look; out-look, distant view, prospect,* 22.

Prō·tinus, adv.· [1 TA-, TEN-], *before one's self; at once, immediately,* 9.

Prō·turbō, 1 [TVR-], *drive forward; drive off, frighten away,* 19. Cf. pellō.

Prō·videō, 2, -vīdī, -vīsum [VID-], *see before; look out, see, attend to,* 22.·

Prō·vincia, -ae, F. [VIC-], *territory acquired by conquest; province,* 29.

Prō·volō, 1, -āvī, —, *fly forth; hasten forth, hurry forward,* 19.

Proximē, adv., superl. of prope [PARC-, PLEC-], *nearest; most, recently, last,* 8, 19.

Proximus, -a, -um, adj. (superl. of propior, no pos.) [PARC-, PLEC-], *nearest, closest,* 3, 12, 33 ; *next, following,* 27, (of time) 12, 35.

Prū·dentia (for prō·videntia), -ae, F. [VID-], *seeing before; foresight, wisdom, prudence,* 4.

Pūblicus, -a, -um, adj. [PLE-,

PLO-], *belonging to the people;* w. rēs, *republic, state, government,* 5.

Puer, -erī, M., *one begotten; boy, child,* 13, 28.

Pūgna, -ae, F. [PAC-, PAG-, PVG-], *thrusting thing; fight, battle,* 16, 25, 28, 29. Cf. proelium.

Pūgnō, 1 [PAC-, PAG-, PVG-], *fight, contend,* 8, 10, 21, 26, 27, 33. Cf. congredior, contendō, dīmicō, proelior.

## Q.

Q., *abbrev. for* Quīntus, 2, 5, 9, 11.

Quā, adv. (abl. F. of quī) [CA-], *on which side; at what point, where,* 33.

Quadrin·gentī, -ae, -a, num. adj [CEN-], *four hundred,* 8.

Quaerō, 3, -sīvī, -sītum, *seek; ask, enquire, make enquiry,* 4, 15 ; *look for, seek, try to find,* 21. Cf. petō.

Quam, adv. (acc. of quī) [CA-], *in what manner; than,* 10, 19, 20, 21, 22, 31, 32. Cf. āc (19).

Quam·vīs, adv. [CA- ; VOL-], *as you will; as much as you like, any-so-ever, any,* 31.

Quantus, -a, -um, adj. [CA-], *how great, how many,* 4, 5, 14, 26, in indir. quest.; *as great as, as much as,* 8, 11. Cf. tantus.

Quartus, -a, -um, adj., *fourth,* 25.

Quattuor, num. adj., indecl., *four,* 33.

Que, enclitic conj. [CA-, CI-], *and,* 1, 2, 3, etc. Joins kindred expressions ; *sometimes* couples a sentence to a preceding one. Cf. et, atque.

**Quī**, quae, quod, rel. and adj. pron. [CA-, CI-], *who, which, what, that,* 1, 2, 3, etc.

**Quī · dam**, quaedam, quoddam, indef. pron. [CA-, CI- ; 3 DA-], *certain one, some one,* 17.

**Qui · dem**, adv. [CA-, CI- ; 3 DA-], *certainly;* nē ... quidem, enclosing emphatic word or expression, *not even,* 3, 17.

**Quī · n**, conj. w. subj. [CA-, CI- ; NA-], *by which not; but that, that, from,* 2, 3.

**Quī · nam** (**quis-**), quae-, quod-, interrog. pron. [CA-, CI-], *for who? who, which, what, pray? what in the world?* 30.

**Quīn · decim**, num. adj., indecl. [DEC-], *fifteen,* 2, 4, 30, 35.

**Quīn · gentī**, -ae, -a, num. adj. [CEN-], *five hundred,* 28.

**Quīnquā · gintā**, num. adj., indecl., *fifty,* 4, 33.

**Quīnque**, num. adj., indecl., *five.*

**Quis**, quae, quid ? interrog. pron. [CA-, CI-], *who? which? what?* 4, 8, 11, etc. Indef. after sī and nē, *any one, any,* 8, 14, 32, 33.

**Quis · quam**, —,quicquam(quidq-), indef. pron. [CA-, CI-], *any, any at all,* 17 ; in negative clauses.

**Quis · que**, quae-, quid- (quod-), indef. pron. [CA-, CI-], *each, each one, every,* 4, 10, 11, 21, 22, 25.

**Quis · quis**, —, quicquid (quidq-) or quodquod, indef. rel. pron. [CA-, CI-], *whatever, whatsoever, everything which,* 17.

**Quō**, rel. adv. (dat. and abl. of quī) [CA-, CI-], *in what place;* (dat. use) *where, whither,* 16, 17, 21 ; conj. (rel. adv.), = ut eō, *by which, so that, that,* 25.

**Quod**, conj. (acc. N. of quī) [CA-, CI-], *that; in that, because,* 1, 4, 10, etc. ; *the fact that,* 17.

**Quo · que**, adv. [CA-, CI-], *also, too, as well,* 10, 22 ; placed after word to be emphasized.

**R.**

**Rāmus**, -ī, M., *growing thing; branch,* 17.

**Ratiō**, -ōnis, F. [RA-], *reckoning; consideration,* 10 ; *plan, method, system,* 19, 22.

**Re-, Red-**, *back, away,* in comp. only.

**Re · cipiō**, **3**, -cēpī, -ceptum [CAP-], *take back; admit, receive,* 3, 15 ; with reflex. pron., *recover,* 12 ; *betake one's self, retreat, go,* 11, 19, 24. Cf. sē cōnferre.

**Red · dō**, **3**, -didī, -ditum [1 DA-], *give back; render,* 5.

**Red · eō**, -īre, -iī, -itum [1 I-], *go back ; recede, decline, slope away,* 8.

**Red · igō**, **3**, -ēgī, -āctum [AG-], *drive back; bring down, reduce,* 14, 28, 34 ; *render,* 27. Cf. reddō.

**Red · in · tegrō**, **1** [TAG-], *make whole again ; renew, restore,* 23, 25, 27.

**Rēdonēs**, -um, M., *tribe of Brittany,* 34.

**Re dūcŏ, 3,-xĭ,** -ductum [DVC-], *lead back*, 9.

**Re·ferŏ,** -ferre, rettulĭ, -lātum [1 FER-], *bear back; report, announce*, 33. Cf. adferŏ, renūntiŏ.

**Re·fringŏ, 3,** -frēgĭ, -frāctum, *break back; break open, tear open*, 33.

**Regiŏ,** -ōnis, F. [REG-], *directing, direction; region, district, locality, country,* 4.

**Rēgnum,** -ĭ, N. [REG-], *that which rules; power, control,* 1.

**Rē·iciŏ, 3,** -iēcĭ, -iectum [IA-, IAC-], *hurl back; throw back, drive back,* 33.

**Re·languēscŏ, 3,** -guĭ,— [LAG-], *lose energy, be weakened,* 15.

**Re·linquŏ, 3,** -līquĭ, -līctum [LIC-, LIQV-] *leave behind, leave,* 5, 8, 29.

**Re·liquus,** -a, -um, adj. [LIC-, LIQV-], *remaining; other, rest of,* 2, 3, 5, etc. ; *as noun,* M., *the rest, the others,* 10, 25.

**Rēmĭ,** -ōrum, M., *people of Belgium on the Axona,* 3, 4, 5, etc.

**Re·mittŏ, 3,** -mīsĭ, -missum [MIT-], *send back; hurl back, return,* 27 ; *relax, weaken,* 15.

**Rēmus,** -ĭ, M., *a Remian,* 6.

**Re·nūntiŏ, 1** [NV-], *bring back word; announce, report,* 24 ; w. dat. and acc. and infin. Cf. adferŏ, referŏ.

**Re·pellŏ, 3,** reppulĭ, -pulsum [PAL-, PEL-, PVL-], *drive back, repulse,* 10. Cf. rēiciŏ.

**Repentīnŏ,** adv. (abl. of repentīnus), *suddenly,* 33.

**Re·periŏ, 4,** repperĭ, -pertụm [2 PAR-, POR-], *produce again ; find, find out, ascertain,* 9 ; w. acc. and infin., 4, 15.

**Rēs,** reĭ, F. [RA-], *thing spoken of; thing, circumstance, matter, affair, business, fact,* 1, 2, 3, etc. ; rēs frūmentāria, *grainsupply, provisions,* 2 ; rēs pūblica, *state, republic,* 5.

**Re·sistŏ, 3,** -stitĭ, — [STA-], *stand back; hold one's ground, maintain one's position, resist,* 22, 23, 26.

**Re·spiciŏ, 3,** -spēxĭ, -spectum [SPEC-], *look back, look behind one,* 24.

**Re·spondeŏ, 2,** -ndĭ, -spōnsum, *promise in return ; reply, answer,* 32.

**Re·tineŏ, 2,** -uĭ, -tentum [1 TA-, TEN-], *keep back ; keep up, maintain,* 21 ; *keep back, reserve,* 32, 33.

**Re·vertor, 3,** -versus (active in perfect, pluperfect, and future perfect: reverti, reverteram, revertero) [VERT-], *turn back; return, go back,* 10, 14, 29, 35.

**Re·vocŏ, 1** (VOC-, VAG-), *call back, summon,* 20.

**Rēx,** rēgis, M. [REG-], *ruler; king, chieftain,* 4, 13.

**Rhēnus,** -ĭ, M., *the Rhine,* 3, 4, 29, 35.

**Rīpa,** -ae, F., *bank, river-bank,* 5, 23, 27.

**Rōmānus,** -a, -um, adj., *Roman,* 1, 3, etc. ; *as noun,* M., *Roman,* 10, 12, 13, etc.

**Rubus, -ī, M.,** *red-colored thing; bramble,* 17.

**Rūmor, -ōris, M.,** *sounding; report, rumor,* 1.

**Rūpēs, -is, F.** [RAP-, RVP-], *broken thing; cliff, steep rock,* 29.

**R·ūrsus, adv.** [VERT-], *turned back; again, back again,* 19, 23, 24.

**S.**

**Sabīnus, -ī, M., Q.** *Titurius Sabinus, lieutenant of Cæsar,* 5.

**Sabis, -is, M.,** *river Sambre in country of Nervii,* 16, 18.

**Saepēs, -is, F.** [1 SAC-, SAG-], *hedge,* 17, 22.

**Sagittārius, -ī, M.** [1 SAC-, SAG-], *of an arrow; archer, bowman,* 7, 10, 19.

**Salūs, -ūtis, F.** [SAL-, SER-], *being well; preservation, salvation, safety,* 27, 33; *well-being, welfare,* 6.

**Sarcinae, -ārum, F.,** *bundle; luggage, personal baggage,* 17.

**Saxum, -ī, N.** [2 SAC-, SEC-], *fragment of rock; rock, stone,* 29.

**Scientia, -ae, F.** [2 SAC-, SEC-, SCI-], *knowing; knowledge,* 20.

**Scrībō, 3, -psī, -ptum** [SCARP-, SCALP-], *scratch; write, give an account,* 29.

**Scūtum, -ī, N.** [SCV-, CV-], *covering thing; shield,* 21, 25, 27, 33.

**Sectiō, -ōnis, F.** [2 SAC-, SEC-], *cutting; lot of booty, booty,* 33.

**Secundum, prep. w. acc.** (acc. N. of secundus) [SEC-], *following; in the direction of, along,* 18.

**Secundus, -a, -um, adj.** [SEC-],

*following; second,* 11; *successful, favorable,* 9.

**Sed, co-ord. conj., adversative** [SOVO-, SVO-], *apart from; but,* 14, 17, 19, 20, 21, 32.

**Senātor, -ōris, M.** [SEN-], *old man; elder, senator,* 28.

**Senātus, -ūs, M.** [SEN-], *office of an old man; council, senate,* 5.

**Senonēs, -um, M.,** *tribe on upper Seine,* 2.

**Sententia, -ae, F.** [SENT-], *thinking; opinion, view,* 10.

**Sentēs, -ium, M.** *thorns, briars, brambles,* 17.

**Septimus, -a, -um, adj.,** *seventh,* 23, 26.

**Sequor, 3, secūtus** [SEC-], *follow; go along, accompany,* 17; *follow, result,* 22.

**Servitūs, -ūtis, F.** [1 SER-, SVAR-], *slavery, servitude, subjection,* 14.

**Servō, 1** [SAL-, SER-], *save; keep, maintain,* 33.

**Sex, num. adj., indecl.,** *six,* 5, 8, 19, 29.

**Sexāgintā, num. adj., indecl.,** *sixty,* 4.

**Sex·centī, -ae, -a, num. adj.** [CEN-], *six hundred,* 15, 28.

**Sī, conj.** [SOVO-, SVO-], *if, in case,* 5, 8, 9, etc.; *to see if, whether,* 9, w. indir. question.

**Sī·c, adv.** [3 SA-; CA-, CI-], *in this manner; so, in such a manner,* 32; *in following manner, as follows,* 4, 15.

**Sīgni·fer, -erī, M.** [3 SAC-; 1 FER-], *standard-bearer, ensign,* 25.

**Signi·ficātiō**, -ōnis, F. [3 SAC-; FAC-], *pointing out; announcement, signal,* 33.

**Signi·ficō, 1** [3 SAC-; FAC-], *show by signs; indicate, show,* 7 ; *announce, make known,* 13 ; w. acc. and infin.

**Signum**, -ī, N. [3 SAC-], *mark; signal, sign,* 20, 21 ; *military standard, ensign,* 21, 25, 26 ; — convertere, *face about, wheel,* 26 ; — īnferre, *advance to attack, charge,* 25 ; ad — cōnsistere, *rally round the standards,* 21.

**Silva**, -ae, F. [2 SER-, SVAL-], *wood, forest,* 18, 19.

**Silvestris**, -e, adj. [2 SER-, SVAL-], *of a wood; wooded,* 18.

**Simul**, adv. [2 SA-, SIM-], *together; at the same time,* 24.

**Si·ne**, prep. w. abl. [SOVO-], *without,* 5, 11, 15, 25, 31.

**Singulāris**, -e, adj. [2 SA-, SEM-, SIM-], *one by one; remarkable, extraordinary,* 24. Cf. eximius.

**Singulī**, -ae, -a, distrib. num. adj. [2 SA-, SEM-, SIM-], *one to each; one at a time, separate, single,* 17, 20.

**Sinister**, -tra, -trum, adj. *left, on the left,* 23.

**Sōl**, -is, M. [2 SER-, SVAL-], *sun,* 11.

**Solli·citō, 1** [SAL-; CI-], *move violently; stir up, instigate, incite,* 1.

**Sōlum**, adv. (acc. N. of sōlus) [SAL-, SER-], *alone, only,* 14.

**Sōlus**, -a, -um, adj. [SAL-, SER-], *alone, only, sole,* 4.

**Spatium**, -ī, N. [SPA-, PA-], *racecourse; space, distance,* 17, 30 ; *extent, time,* 11.

**Speciēs**, -iēī, F. [SPEC-], *seeing; sight, form, appearance,* 31.

**Speculātor**, -ōris, M. [SPEC-], *searcher; scout, spy,* 11. Cf. explōrātor.

**Spēs**, -eī, F. [SPA, PA-], *hope, expectation,* 7, 25, 27, 33.

**Spīritus**, -ūs, M., *breathing; feeling, pride, haughtiness,* 4.

**Statim**, adv. [STA-], *in standing; at once, immediately,* 11. Cf. prōtinus.

**Statiō**, -ōnis, F. [STA-], *standing; guard, out-post, picket,* 18.

**Statuō, 3**, -uī, -ūtum [STA-], *make stand; fix, determine, decide,* 8, 31.

**Statūra**, -ae, F. [STA-], *standing upright; stature, size,* 30.

**Strepitus**, -ūs, M., *clashing, clatter, noise, din,* 11. Cf. clāmor, fremitus.

**Studeō, 2**, -uī, — [SPA-, PA-], *be eager; strive after, be bent upon, desire,* 1 ; *devote one's self to, pay attention to,* 17 ; w. dat.

**Studium**, -ī, N. [SPA-, PA-], *zeal, eagerness, enthusiasm,* 7.

**Sub**, prep. w. abl. and acc., *under, beneath* 17; *near to, toward,* 11, 33.

**Sub·eō**, -īre, -iī, -itum [1 I-], *go under; go near, approach closely, come up,* 25, 27. Cf. adpropinquō, succēdō.

**Sub·itō**, adv. (abl. of subitus) [1 I-], *by coming on stealthily; suddenly, unexpectedly,* 19 ; *hastily, offhand,* 33. Cf. repentīnō.

**Sub·mittō (summ-), 3,** -mīsī, -missum [MIT-], *send below; send to aid, despatch, send,* 6, 25 ; w. dat.

**Sub·ruō (surr-), 3,** -ruī, -rutum, *tear down below; undermine, dig under,* 6.

**Sub·sequor, 3,** -secūtus [SEC-], *follow closely, pursue,* 11, 19.

**Sub·sidium,** -ī, N. [SED-], *sitting behind; reserve forces, reserves,* 22, 25 ; *aid, assistance, help,* 6, 7, 8, 20, 26. Cf. auxilium.

**Suc·cēdō (subc-), 3,** -cessī, -cessum [CAD-], *go below; draw near, approach closely,* 6. Cf. subeō, adpropīnquō.

**Suc·cessus (subc-),** -ūs, M. [CAD-], *going below; advance, close approach,* 20.

**Suessiōnēs,** -um, M., *German tribe north of the Marne,* 3, 4, 12, 13.

**Suī,** sibi, sē (sēsē), reflex. pron. *referring to subject or speaker,* [SOVO-, SVO-], *self; of himself, of themselves, etc.,* 1, 2, 3, etc.

**Sum,** esse, fuī [ES-], *be; exist, be,* 1, 2, 3, etc.

**Summa,** -ae, F. (F. of summus, sc. rēs), *highest (thing); chief control, general management,* 4, 23.

**Summus,** -a, -um, adj. (superl. of superus), *highest, greatest, topmost,* 6, 23, 24, 32 ; *highest part, summit, top,* 18, 26.

**Sū·mō, 3,** -mpsī, -mptum [EM-], *take, claim, assume,* 4.

**Superior,** -ius, gen. -ōris, adj. compar. of superus, *higher, up-*

per, 18, 23, 26 ; *preceding, former, past,* 20. Cf. altior ; prīstinus.

**Superō, 1,** *go over; defeat, vanquish,* 24. Cf. vincō.

**Super·sedeō, 2,** -sēdī, -sessum [SED-], *sit over; refrain from, omit, postpone,* 8 ; w. abl.

**Super·sum,** -esse, -fuī [ES-], *be above; remain, survive,* 27, 28.

**Sup·plex (subpl-),** -icis, adj. [PARC-, PLEC-], *folding the knees beneath; suppliant, beseeching,* 28.

**Sup·plicātiō (subpl-)** -ōnis, F. [PARC-, PLEC-], *kneeling down; thanksgiving,* 35.

**Suprā,** adv., *on upper side; above, before,* 1, 18, 29.

**Sus·tentō, 1** [1 TA-, TEN-], *keep holding up; hold out, maintain one's self,* 6, 14.

**Sus·tineō, 2,** -uī, -tentum [1 TA-, TEN-], *hold up under; withstand, sustain,* 11, 21 ; with reflex. pron., *hold out,* 6 ; *keep upright, stand up,* 25.

**Suus,** -a, -um, poss. adj. [SOVO-, SVO-], *of himself, his own, their own, etc.,* 3, 4, 5, etc. ; as noun, M., *their (his) countrymen, friends,* 6, 8, 9, etc. ; N., *property, possessions,* 3, 13, 29.

**T.**

**T.,** praenomen *Titus, T. Labienus,* 11, 26.

**Tam,** adv. [2 TA-], *so far; so, to such a degree,* 21.

**Tamen,** adv. [2 TA-], *in so far; still, however; nevertheless,* 8, 32.

**Tantulus**, -a, -um, dim. adj. [2 TA-], *so small; so trifling*, 30. Cf. parvulus.

**Tantus**, -a, -um, adj. [2 TA-], *of such size; so great, so much*, 3, 5, 6, etc.

**Tardō, 1**, *make slow, retard, check*, 25.

**Tardus**, -a, -um, adj., *slow (weary, exhausted)*, 25.

**Tegimenta** (**tegu-**), -ōrum, N., *means of covering; covering, cover*, 21.

**Tēlum**, -ī, N. [TEC-], *missile, weapon, javelin*, 6, 10, 21, 25, 27, 33.

**Tempus**, -oris, N. [1 TA-, TEN-], *time* (in general), 5, 14, 19, 20, 21, 24, 33, 34 ; *moment*, 19 ; *time, period, day*, 17, 35 ; *emergency, crisis*, 22.

**Tendō, 3**, tetendī, tentum (tēnsum) [1 TA-, TEN-], *stretch; stretch out, extend*, 13. Cf. pandō.

**Teneō, 2**, -uī, — [1 TA-, TEN-], *hold, have*, 23; *hold, surround*, 24.

**Tener**, -era, -erum, adj. [1 TA-, TEN-], *tender, young*, 17.

**Terror**, -ōris, M. [TER-, TERS-], *frightening; great fear, fright, panic*, 12.

**Tertius**, -a, -um, adj., *third*, 1, 32, 33.

**Testūdō**, -inis, F., *having a shell; tortoise, bulwark of shields*, 6.

**Teutonī**, -ōrum (-ēs, -um), M., *German tribe*, 4, 29.

**Timeō, 2**, -uī, —, *fear, be afraid, entertain fears*, 26, w. nē followed by subjunctive.

**Titurius**, -ī, M., *Q. Titurius Sabinus, lieutenant of Cæsar's*, 5, 9, 10.

**Titus**, -ī, M., *praenomen of Labienus, Cæsar's lieutenant*, 11, 26.

**Tormentum**, -ī, N. [TARC- (TARP-), TREP-], *thing twisted; machine of war, engine for hurling*, 8.

**Tot·idem**, adj., indecl. [2 TA-; 3 DA], *just as many, same number of*, 4.

**Tōtus**, -a, -um, gen. totīus, adj. [TV-, TO-], *increased; whole, entire*, 4, 6, 19, 23.

**Trabs**, trabis, F. [TARC- (TARP-), TREP-], *beam, timber*, 29.

**Trā·dō, 3**, -didī, -ditum [1 DA-], *give over; hand over, give up, surrender*, 13, 15, 31, 32.

**Trā·dūcō, 3**, -xī, -ductum [DVC-], *lead over; lead across, bring over*, 4, 5, 9, 10.

**Trāns**, prep. w. acc., *across, over, beyond*, 16, 35.

**Trāns·eō**, -īre, -iī, -itum [1 I-], *go over; go across, cross*, 9, 10, 23, 24, 27.

**Trāns·gredior, 3**, -gressus [GRAD-], *go, over; go across, cross*, 19. Cf. trānseō.

**Trāns·versus**, -a, -um, adj. [VERT-], *turned across; crosswise, at right angles, oblique*, 8.

**Trēs**, tria, gen. -ium, num. adj., *three*, 11, 18, 28, 33.

**Trēverī**, -ōrum, M., *Celtic tribe on the Moselle*, 24.

**Tribūnus**, -ī, M., *tribune*, 26.

**Trī·duum**, -ī, N. [DIV-, DI-, DIAV-], *three days' time*, 16.

**Tuba**, -ae, F., *trumpet*, 20.

**Tum**, adv. [2 TA-], *then, at that time*, 2, 6; *then, in addition, further*, 27, 29; cum . . . tum, *both . . . and*, 4.

**Tumultus**,- ūs, M. [TV-, TVM-], *swelling; confusion, uproar, noise*, 11. Cf. strepitus.

**Tumulus**, -ī, M. [TV-, TVM-], *swelling up; mound, hillock, hill*, 27.

**Turonēs**, -um (-ī, -ōrum), M., *tribe of Gaul on Loire*, 35.

**Turpitūdō**, -inis, F. [TARC- (TARP-), TREP-], *ugliness; disgrace, dishonor*, 27.

**Turris**, -is, F. [TVR-], *tower*, 12, 30, 33.

**Tūtus**, -a, -um, adj. (P. of tueor), *well guarded; safe, secure*, 5, 28.

### U.

**Ubi**, rel. adv. [CA-, CI-], *in which place; where*, 8, 35; *when, as soon as*, 6, 8, 9, 10, 19, 25, 30, 31.

**Ūllus**, -a, -um, gen. ūllīus, dim. adj. [2 I-], *any one (at all), any*, 11, 15, 25; w. negative expression.

**Ūnā**, adv. (abl. F. of ūnus) [2 I-], *in one and the same place; at the same time, together*, 16, 17, 24, 28, 29; foll. by cum. and abl.

**Ūn·decimus**, -a, -um, adj. [2 I-; DEC-], *eleventh*, 23.

**Undi·que**, adv. [CA-, CI-], *whencesoever; from every quarter, from all sides*, 6, 10.

**Unelli**, -ōrum, M., *tribe in Normandy*, 34.

**Ūni·versus**, -a, -um, adj. [2 I-; VERT-], *turned into one; whole, all, in a mass*, 33.

**Ūnus**, -a, -um, gen. -īus, num. adj. [2 I-], *one*, 2, 5, 6, 29, 31, 34; *one, one and the same*, 3, 5, 19, 20; *common, one alone*, 4, 22; *alone, only*, 33; *a*, 25.

**Urgeō**, 2, ursī, — [VERG-, VRG-], *press, press hard*, 25, 26.

**Ūsus**, -ūs, M. [1 AV-], *using; practice, experience*, 20; *use, advantage*, 9, 12.

**Ut** or **Utī**, conj. [CA-, CI-], *in what manner; as*, 1, 7, 11, etc., w. indic.; *in order that, that, to*, 2, 8, 9, etc.; *that, so that*, 3, 4, 5, etc.

**Uter·que**, -traque, -trumque, gen. utrīusque, pron. [CA-, CI-], *both one and the other; each of two, both*, 8, 16, 25.

**Ūtor**, 3, ūsus [1 AV-], *use, make use of, employ, have*, 3, 7, 10, 25, 28; *use, practise*, 14, 28; *enjoy, maintain*, 32; w. abl.

### V.

**Vacuus**, -a, -um, adj., *empty, clear, free, unoccupied;* w. ab and abl., 12.

**Vadum**, -ī, N. [BA-, VA-], *place through which one can go; ford, crossing*, 9.

**Valeō**, 2, -uī, -itūrus, *be strong, have influence*, 4, 17.

**Vallum**, -ī, N. [1 VEL-, VAL-], *earthen wall; earth-works, rampart*, 5, 30, 33.

**Varius**, -a, -um, adj., *spotted; changing, different*, 22.

**Vāstō, 1,** *make empty; lay waste, ravage.* Cf. populor, dēpopulor.

**Velocassēs, -um, M.,** *one of the minor Belgian tribes,* 4.

**Vēn·dō, 3,** -didī (-ditum) [1 DA-], *place for sale; sell,* 33.

**Venellī,** see **Unellī.**

**Venetī, -ōrum, M.,** *tribe of Bretagne,* 34.

**Veniō, 4,** vēnī, ventum [BA-, VA-, VEN-], *come, approach,* 2, 3, 5, etc.

**Verbum, -ī, N.** [VER-], *that spoken; word, discourse, intercession,* 14.

**Vereor, 2** [1 VEL-, VER-], *feel awe; fear, be afraid,* 11.

**Vergō, 3, —, —** [VERG-], *bend, incline,* 18.

**Vērō, adv.** (abl. N. of vērus) [VER-], *in truth, in fact, but, however,* 2, 27, 31.

**Veromanduī, -ōrum, M.,** *Gallic tribe in modern Picardy,* 4, 16, 23.

**Versō, 1** [VERT-], *keep turning;* pass., *be engaged in, be occupied about,* 24 ; *dwell, remain, be,* 1.

**Vesper, -erī** or **-eris, M.,** *evening, nightfall,* 33.

**Vester, -tra, -trum,** *your, yours.*

**Vetō, 1,** -uī, -itum [VET-], *leave in old state; advise against, forbid,* 20.

**Vēxillum, -ī, N.** [VAG-, VEH-], *military ensign, banner, flag,* 20.

**Vēxō, 1** [VAG-, VEH-], *keep carrying; harass, overrun,* 4.

**Victor, -ōris, M.** [VIC-], *conqueror, victor,* 28 ; in appos. *conquering, victorious,* 24.

**Vīcus, -ī, M.,** *row of houses; village, hamlet,* 7.

**Videō, 2,** vīdī, vīsum [VID-], *see, perceive,* 12, 19 ; *see, know,* 5, 10, 24, 25, 26, 30, 31, w. acc. and infin. ; pass., *seem, appear,* 11, 16, 18, 28, 33 ; *seem good, seem best,* 20.

**Vigilia, -ae, F.,** *being awake; watch, night-watch,* 11, 33.

**Vīmen, -inis, N.** [VI-, VIC-], *means of binding; willow, withe, wicker-work,* 33.

**Vincō, 3,** vīcī, victum [VIC-], *conquer, defeat,* 28. Cf. superō.

**Vīnea, -ae, F.** [VI-, VIC-], *shelter for vines; covered shed, movable shelter,* 12, 30.

**Vīnum, -ī, N.** [VI-, VIC-], *wine,* 15.

**Vir, virī, M.,** *male, man,* 25, 33.

**Virtūs, -ūtis, F.,** *manhood; bravery, valor,* 4, 8, 15, 21, 24, 27, 31, 33.

**Vīs, vim, vī, F.,** *strength, power,* 30.

**Vītō, 1,** *shun, try to escape, avoid,* 25.

**Vix, adv.** [VIC-], *with effort; barely, scarcely, hardly,* 28.

**Voluntās, -ātis, F.** [VOL-], *will, wish, desire,* 4.

**Vōx, vōcis, F.** [VOC], *that which calls out; voice, utterance,* 13, 30.

**Vulgō (volgō), adv.** (abl. of vulgus) [VERG-, VALG-], *among the people; generally, commonly,* 1.

**Vulnerō, 1** [2 VEL-, VOL-], *wound, injure,* 25.

**Vulnus, -eris, N.** [2 VEL-, VOL-], *wound, hurt,* 23, 25, 27.

# ETYMOLOGICAL VOCABULARY.

The relation in meaning of some of the words in certain groups to the root is sometimes obscure or even impossible to be traced with absolute certainty. Sometimes the relation is obscured by the omission in this vocabulary of an interlinking word, because it does not occur in the text. Let us take an example close at hand, the root AID- and the noun aestuārium. The notion "inlet" seems very remote from the notion "burn." But aestuārium is formed from aestus (for *aedtus*), the first meaning of which is *the raging of fire, waves or billows of heat.* As we might expect, a secondary meaning is, *the raging of water, waves, billows,* in the proper sense. From the force of the suffix -ārium, aestuārium should mean a *sea-marsh,* or *a tract overflowed at high tide;* and from this the notion "inlet," the place through which the tide rushes, comes naturally enough.

The following roots, with their meanings, have been mostly taken from the excellent Elementary Latin Dictionary of Dr. Charlton T. Lewis.

1. AC-, sharp, pierce.
Aciēs, edge, line of battle.
Prae·acūtus, sharpened at the point.
Ācr·iter, sharply.
Acervus, heap.
Co·acervō, heap up.

2. AC-, swift.
Equēs, horseman.
Equester, of horsemen.
Equitātus, cavalry.

AG-, drive.
Agō, drive, lead.
Cō·gō [for con·agō], drive together, compel.
Red·igō, drive back, reduce.
Ager, land.
Agmen, marching column.
Ignis, fire.
Ex·agitō, harass.

AID-, burn.
Aedi·ficium [from aedēs, hearth], building.
Aestās [for aid·tās], summer.
Aestuārium [for aid·t-], inlet.

1. AL-, AR-, feed, grow, raise.
Altus, high.
Altitūdō, height.
Arduus, steep.
Arbor, tree.

2. AL- (ALI-), other, strange.
Alius, other.
Aliās, at some other time.
Aliēnus, another's.
Al·iter, other-wise.
Alter, the other (of two).

AM-, love.
Amīcus, friend.
Amīcitia, friendship.
In·imīcus, unfriendly, hostile.

**AN-**, breathe.
**Animus**, spirit.
**Ex·animō**, make breathless.
**Onus** (as the cause of panting), weight.

**ANA-**, pronominal stem, third person.
**In**, in, into.
**Inter**, between.
**Inter·eā**, meanwhile.
**Inter·im**, meanwhile.
**Interior** [compar. of obs. *interus*], inner.
**Intrā**, within.
**Intrō**, enter.
**?Ille** [old form *ollus*, from *onolus*], that one.

**ANT-**, before, against.
**Ante**, before, formerly.
**Antīquitus**, of old.

**AP-, OP-**, lay hold of work, help.
**(Ops)**, aid.
**Opus**, work.
**Opera**, exertion, service.
**C·ōpia** [for *com·opia*], supply.
**Co·epī** [for *com·apiō*], begin.
**Optimus**, best.
**Omnis** [for *apnis*], all.
**Opīniō**, impression.

**APA-**, *away, from.*
**Ab**, from, by.
**Ap·ud**, among.
**Ob**, against.

**AR-**, fit.
**Armō**, arm.
**Arma**, arms.
**Armātūra**, equipment.
**In·ermis**, unarmed.

**ARC-**, shut in, keep off.
**Ex·ercitus**, army.
**Ex·ercitātus**, trained.

1. **AV-**, mark, desire, delight.
**Audeō**, dare.
**Audāc·ter**, boldly.

**Ūtor** [for *avitor*], use.
**Ūsus**, use, experience.
**In·ūsitātus**, unusual.
**In·ūtilis**, useless.
**Neg·ōtium** [for *nec·avtium*], business.

2. **AV-**, mark, notice.
**Audiō**, hear.
**Ex·audiō**, overhear.

**AVG-**, grow.
**Auctōritās**, power.
**Auxilium**, aid.

**BA-, VA-, VEN-**, go.
**Ar·bitror** [for *ad·batror*], believe.
**Du·bitō**, doubt, hesitate.
**Vadum**, ford.
**Veniō**, come.
**Ad·ventus**, arrival.
**Circum·veniō**, outflank.
**Con·veniō**, meet.
**Dē·veniō**, come to.

Ē·ventus, outcome.
In·veniō, find.
Ob·veniō, fall in with.
Per·veniō, arrive at.

CA-, CI-, pronominal stem, who.
Quī, who.
Quī·dam, a certain one.
Qui·dem, certainly.
Quīn [for quī·nē], but that.
Quā, where.
Quō, whither.
Quod, because.
Quis, who?
Quī·nam, who, pray?
Quis·quam, any.
Nē·quī·quam, in vain.
Quis·quis, whoever.
Quis·que, each one.
Quo·que, also.
Cum (quom), when.
Quam, than.
Quam·vīs, how-so-ever.
Post·quam, after.
Prius·quam, sooner than.
Quantus, how great.
Que, and.
Ita·que, and so.
Ne·que, and not.
Ubi [for quō·bi], where.
Undi·que [for cunde·que], from all sides.

Cēterī, the others.
Cis, this side of.
Citerior, hither.
Citrā, this side of.

Ut or Utī [for cutī or quotī], as, in order that.
Uter·que [for quoter·que], each.
Ne·uter, neither.

Cotī·diē, daily.
Hī·c [for hi·ce], this.
Nun·c [for num·ce], now.
Sī·c [for si·ce], so.

CAD-, fall.
Cadō, fall.
Ac·cidō (adc-), befall.
In·cidō, happen.
Cadāver, dead body.
Cāsus, happening.
Oc·cāsus (obc-), setting.
Cēdō, give way.
Ac·cēdō (adc-), approach.
Dis·cēdō, depart.
Dis·cessus, departure.
Ex·cēdō, withdraw from.
Inter·cēdō, intervene.
Prō·cēdō, advance.
Suc·cēdō (subc-), approach.
Suc·cessus (subc-), close approach.
Ar·cessō [for ad·cēdsō], summon.

1. CAL-, CAR-, call.
Con·cilium, meeting.
Clāmor, shouting.

2. CAL-, SCAL-, cover, hide.
Oc·cultus (obc-), hidden.
Galea, helmet.
Domi·cilium, dwelling-place.
Cēlō, hide.

CAP-, take, hold.
**Ac · cĭpĭŏ (adc-)**, receive.
**In · cĭpĭŏ**, begin.
**Inter · cĭpĭŏ**, intercept.
**Re · cĭpĭŏ**, receive.
**Captīvus**, captive.

**Oc · cŭpŏ (obc-)**, take into pos-
    session.
**Caput**, head.
**Prae · ceps**, headlong.
**Prīn · ceps**, leader.

CAR-, SCAR-, hard, scrape.
**Cortex**, bark.
**Cornū**, horn, wing.

CAV-, watch.
**Causa**, cause.
**In · cūsŏ**, accuse.

CEL-, CER-, strike, drive.
**Gladius** [for *cladius*], sword.
**Celeritās**, swiftness.
**Celer · ĭter**, swiftly.
**Pro · cul**, at a distance.
**Cursus**, running.
**Con · currŏ**, run together.
**Dē · currŏ**, run down.
**Oc · currŏ (obc-)**, meet.
**Ex · cursĭŏ**, sally.

CEN-, hundred.
**Centum**, hundred.
**Centurĭŏ**, centurion.
**Du · centī**, two hundred.
**Quadrin · gentī**, four hundred.
**Quīn · gentī**, five hundred.
**Sex · centī**, six hundred.

1. CER-, CRE-, make.
**Crēber**, numerous.
**Corpus**, body.

2. CER-, CRE-, part.
**Dē · cernŏ**, decide upon.
**Dē · certŏ**, fight decisively.
**Certus**, sure.

CI-, rouse.
**In · cĭtŏ**, urge on.
**Solli · cĭtŏ (sōli-)**, stir up.

CLĪ-, lean.
**Clē · mentia**, mildness.
**Ad · clīvis (acc-)**, sloping up-
    ward.
**Ad · clīvitās (acc-)**, upward
    slope.
**Dē · clīvis**, sloping downward.

CRAT-, faith.
**Crē · do**, [for *crat · dŏ*], believe.
**In · crē · dĭbĭlis** [for *in · crat · dĭ-
    bĭlis*], incredible.

CVR-, CIR-, curve.
**Circum**, around.
**Circĭ · ter**, about.
**Circu · ĭtus**, circumference.
**Cruciātus**, torture.

1. DA-, give.
**Dŏ**, give.
**Dē · dŏ**, give up.
**Dē · ditĭcius**, one who has sur-
    rendered.
**Dē · ditĭŏ**, surrender.
**Ē · ditus** [P. of *ē · dŏ*], rising.

**Red·dŏ**, give back.
**Trā·dŏ** [for *trāns·dŏ*], give over.
**Vĕn·dŏ** [for *vēnum·dŏ*], sell.

2. DA-, put.
**Ab·dŏ**, hide.
**Crĕ·dŏ**, believe.
**In·crĕ·dibilis**, incredible.
**Man·dŏ**, commission.

3. DA-, pronominal stem, third person.
**Ī·dem**, the same.
**Quī·dam**, a certain one.
**Qui·dem**, indeed.
**Tot·idem**, just as many.

DEC-, ten.
**Decem**, ten.
**Decimus**, tenth.
**Decumānus** (deci-), of the tenth (cohort), in the phrase, *porta decumāna*, the main entrance to a Roman camp.
**Ūn·decimus**, eleventh.
**Duo·decimus**, twelfth.
**Quīn·decim**, fifteen.

DĪC-, DIĊ- (DAC-), show, point.
**Dīcŏ**, say.
**Doceŏ**, teach.
**Iū·dicŏ**, judge.
**(Diciŏ)**, control.
**Con·diciŏ**, condition.

DIV-, DI-, DIAV-, shine.
**Dīvīnus**, divine.

**Diĕs**, day.
**Cotī·diĕ**, daily.
**Postrī·diĕ** [for *posterō diē*], next day.
**Trī·duum**, three days' time.
**Dum** [for *dium*], while.
**Nōn·dum**, not yet.
**Diū**, for a long time.
**Iuvŏ**, [for *diuvō*], aid.
**Ad·iuvŏ**, aid.

DOM-, build.
**Domus**, home.
**Domi·cilium**, dwelling-place.
**Domesticus**, of home.

DVA-, DVI-, apart, two.
**Duo**, two.
**Duo·decimus**, twelfth.
**Duo·dē·vīgintī**, eighteen.
**Du·bitŏ**, doubt, hesitate.
**Du·centī**, two hundred.
**Du·plex**, two-fold.
**Bellum** [for *duellum*], war.

DVC-, lead.
**Dux**, leader.
**Dūcŏ**, lead.
**Ad·dūcŏ**, bring to.
**Con·dūcŏ**, gather.
**Dē·dūcŏ**, lead off.
**Ē·dūcŏ**, lead out.
**In·dūcŏ**, cover.
**Intrō·dūcŏ**, lead in.
**Ob·dūcŏ**, extend.
**Re·dūcŏ**, lead back.
**Trā·dūcŏ** [for *trāns·dūcō*], lead across.

EM-, take.
Emō, buy.
Ex·imius, excellent.
Sū·mō [for sub·imō], take.

ES-, be, live.
Sum [for esum], be.
Ab·sum, be away.
Dē·sum, be lacking.
Inter·sum, be between.
Prae·sum, command,
Super·sum, survive.

FAC-, put, make.
Faciō, do.
Fīō, passive of faciō, become.
Cōn·ficiō, accomplish, wear out.
Dē·ficiō, fail.
Ef·ficiō, bring about.
Inter·ficiō, kill.
Pate·faciō, throw open.
Prae·ficiō, place in command.
Prō·ficīscor, put one's self forward, set out.
Prō·fectiō, setting out.
Facilis, easy.
Facile, easily.
Aedi·ficium, building.
Ampli·ficō, enlarge.
Dif·ficilis (disf-), difficult.
Dif·ficultās (disf-), difficulty.
Facultās, opportunity.
Male·ficium, outrage.
Sīgni·ficō, announce.
Sīgni·ficātiō, signal.

FEN-, FEND-, strike.
Dē·fendō, ward off, defend.

Dē·fēnsiō, defence.
Dē·fēnsor, defender.

1. FER-, bear.
Ferō, bear,
Ad·ferō (aff-), bring to.
Cōn·ferō, bring together.
Dē·ferō, carry.
In·ferō, bring upon.
Of·ferō (obf-), carry.
Per·ferō, endure.
Prae·ferō, place before, out-do.
Re·ferō, bring back.
Fertilitās, fertility.
Ferāx, fertile.
Fōrs, chance.
Fōrtūna, fortune.
Sīgni·fer, standard-bearer.

2. FER-, FRE-, hold, fix.
Ferē, almost.
Cōn·firmō, give assurance, re-assure.
Fortis [for forctis], brave.
Fort·iter, bravely,

1. FID-, FĪD-, bind, trust.
Fidēs, faith.
Cōn·fīdō, trust.

2. FID-, split.
Fīnis [for fidnis], limit.
Fīnitimus, neighboring.
Ad·fīnitās, connection by marriage.

FLAG-, FLIG-, strike.
Cōn·flīgō, contend with.
Prō·flīgō, defeat.

1. FVG-, FRVG-, use, enjoy.
Frūmentum [for *frūgimentum*],
grain.
Frūmentārius, of grain.

2. FVG-, bend, flee.
Fuga, flight.
Fugiō, flee.
Pro · fugiō, flee.

FVR-, FERV-, rage, swell.
Furor, frenzy.
?Frōns, front.

GEN-, GN-, GNA-, beget.
Nāscor (gn-), arise.
Ē · nāscor, grow out.
Nātus, birth.
Nātiō, nation.
Nātūra, nature.
Prō · gnātus, sprung from.

GER-, carry.
Gerō, carry on.
Ag · ger (adg-), mound.

GNA-, GNO-, know.
Nam, for.
Nāvō [for *gnāvō*], perform with
knowledge and zeal.
Cō · gnōscō, learn.
Nōbilitās, high birth.
Nōmen, name.
Nōminātim, by name.
Nōminō, mention.

GRAD-, walk.
Ad · gredior (agg-), attack.
Con · gredior, meet.
Ē · gredior, go from.
In · gredior, enter.

Prō · gredior, advance.
Trāns · gredior, cross.

HAB-, have.
Habeō, have.
Dē · beō [for de · hibeō], owe to.
Prae · beō [for prae · hibeō], furnish.
Pro · hibeō, restrain.

HAM-, man.
Homō, man.
Nē · mō [for ne · homō], nobody.

HĪM-, cold.
Hiemō, pass the winter.
Hībernus [for *hiemernus*], of
winter.
Hībernācula, winter quarters.

1. I-, AI-, go.
Ad · eō, approach.
Ad · itus, approach.
Circu · itus [for circum · itus], cir-
cumference.
Ex · eō, go forth, set out.
In · eō, enter upon.
In · itium, beginning.
Ob · itus, destruction.
Red · eō, return.
Sub · eō, approach closely.
Sub · itō, suddenly.
Trāns · eō, cross.
Iter, route.
Aetās [for aevitās], age.
   From iter is the adv., ending -iter
   or -ter, as in aequāl · iter for
   aequale · iter, al · iter, audāc · -
   ter, celer · iter, circi · ter, dili-
   gent · (t)er, fort · iter, lēn · iter,
   in · diligent · (t)er.

**2. I-, AI-,** pronominal stem, third person, demonstrative.

**Is,** this one.
**Eŏ,** there.
**Inter · eā,** meanwhile.
**Inter · im,** meanwhile.
**Post · eā,** afterwards.
**Propter · eā,** for the reason (that).
**Ī · dem,** the same.
**Iden · t · idem** [for *idem · et · idem*], again and again.
**I · pse,** self.
**Ibĭ,** there.
**Inde,** thence.
**De · inde,** thereupon.
**Ita,** thus.
**Ita · que,** therefore.
**Item,** likewise.
**?I · dŏneus,** suitable.

**Ūnus** [for *oenus*], one.
**Ūnā,** together.
**Ūni · versus,** all.
**Ūn · decimus,** eleventh.
**Ūllus** [for *ūnulus*], any.
**Nūllus** [for *ne · ūnulus*], none.
**Nŏn · nūllus,** some.
**Nŏn** [*ne · oenum (ūnum)*], not.
**Nŏn · dum,** not yet.

**IA-, IAC-,** go, send.
**Iaciŏ,** throw.
**Ad · iciŏ,** hurl.
**Circum · iciŏ,** place around.
**Cŏn · iciŏ,** hurl.
**Dē · iciŏ,** throw down from.
**Dē · iectus,** slope.
**Inter · iciŏ,** place between.

**Prŏ · iciŏ,** hurl.
**Rĕ · iciŏ,** hurl back.
**Iaceŏ,** lie.

**IC-, AIC-,** like.
**Aequāl · iter,** evenly.
**Ad · aequŏ,** equal.
**In · īquus,** unfavorable.
**In · īquitās,** inequality.

**IV-, IVG-,** bind, yoke.
**Iugum,** ridge.
**Con · iungŏ,** join together.
**Cūnctus** [for *cŏn · iūnctus*], all.
**Iūs,** right.
**Iūstitia,** justice.
**Con · iūrŏ,** conspire.
**In · iūria,** wrong.
**Iū · dicŏ,** judge.
**Iubeŏ,** order.
**Iūxtā** [for *iŭgistā*], close by.

**LAG-,** loose.
**Re · languēscŏ,** lose energy.
**Lassitūdŏ,** exhaustion.
**Laxŏ,** widen.

**1. LEG-, LIG-,** gather.
**Dē · ligŏ,** choose.
**Dī · ligen · ter** [for *dis · ligent · ter*], scrupulously.
**In · dī · ligen · ter,** carelessly.
**Ē · ligŏ,** choose.
**Intel · legŏ,** understand.
**Legiŏ,** legion.
**Legiōnārius,** of a legion.

**2. LEG-,** run, spring.
**Levis** [for *legvis*], light.
**Levitās,** lightness.

Longus, long.
Longē, far.

3. LEG-, lie, be fixed.
Lēx, law.
Lēgātus, envoy.
Lēgātiō, embassy.

LI-, pour, smear.
Littera, written character.
Dē·leō, destroy.

LIB-, desire.
Līberī, children (the free).
Līberāl·iter, generously.

LIC-, LIQV-, let, leave.
Pol·liceor [for prō·liceor], promise.
Re·linquō, leave behind.
Re·liquus, remaining.

1. MA-, MAN-, measure.
Manus, hand.
Man·dō [for manus·dō], commission.
Mani·pulus, handful, maniple.
Mān·suētūdō, gentleness.
Dī·mētior, measure out.
Mōs, custom.

2. MA-, MAD-, measure, moderate.
Modus, manner.
Modo, only.
Com·modē (conm-), easily.
Ad·com·modō (acconm-), fit.

MAC-, MAG-, big.
Magis [for magius], more.

Māximē, most.
Māgnus, great.
Māgnitūdō, greatness.
Māior [for magior], greater.
Magistrātus, office.
Molestē, in a troublesome manner.

MAL-, crush, grind.
Male·ficium, outrage.
Mulier, woman.

1. MAN-, MEN-, man, mind, stay.
Moneō, advise.
Dē·mōnstrō, point out.
Clē·mentia, kindness.

2. MAN-, MI-, small, less.
Minor, smaller.
Minus, less.
Minimē, least.
Ad·ministrō, execute.

MĪL-, associate.
Mīlle, thousand.
Mīles, soldier.
Mīlitāris, of war.

MIS-, wretched.
Miser, wretched.
Miseri·cordia, pity.

MIT-, send, throw.
Mittō, send.
Ā·mittō, lose.
Com·mittō (conm-), join together.
Dī·mittō, despatch.
Ē·mittō, let fly.

Inter · mittŏ, halt.
Intrŏ · mittŏ, send in.
O · mittŏ [for *ob · mittō*], neglect.
Per · mittŏ, grant.
Prae · mittŏ, send in advance.
Re · mittŏ, send back.
Sub · mittŏ, send as aid.

1. MV-, MOV-, move.
Moveŏ, move.
Com · moveŏ, startle.
Per · moveŏ, rouse.
Prŏ · moveŏ, move forward.
Mŏbilĭtās, nimbleness.
Com · mūtātĭŏ, change.

2. MV-, shut, fasten.
Com · mūnis (conm-), common.
Moenia, walls.
Mūnĭŏ, fortify.
Circum · mūnĭŏ, blockade.
Mūnĭmentum, fortification.
Mūnītĭŏ, fortification.
Mūrus [old *moerus*], wall.

NA-, no.
Nĕ, that not, lest.
Ne · que, and not.
Nĕ · ve or Neu, and that not.
Nĭ · hĭl, nothing.
Nĭ · si [for *nĕ · si*], if not.
Nŏn [for *ne · oenum* (*ūnum*)], not.
Nŏn · dum, not yet.
Quĭn [for *qui · nĕ*], but that.

1. NEC-, NOC-, kill, hurt.
Inter · necĭŏ, annihilation.
Nox, night.
Noctŭ, by night.

2. NEC-, bind.
Necessĭtās, necessity.
Necessārĭus, necessary.

NV-, now (pronominal stem).
Noster, our.
Nunc [for *num · ce*], now.
Novus, new, fresh.
Nūntĭus [for *noventius*, from obs. *noveō*, from *novus*], messenger.
Nūntĭŏ, report.
Re · nūntĭŏ, report.

OL-, OR-, grow, rise.
Orĭor, arise.
Ad · orĭor, assault.
Ōrdŏ, order.

PA-, feed.
Pater, father.
Patrĭus, ancestral.
Pābulum, fodder.

PAC-, PAG-, PVG-, fix, peg.
Pāx, peace.
Pācŏ, subdue.

Pūgnŏ, fight.
Ex · pūgnŏ, storm.
Op · pūgnŏ (obp-), assault.
Op · pūgnātĭŏ (obp-), assault.
Prŏ · pūgnŏ, defend.

PAL-, PEL-, PVL-, drive, scatter.
Pellŏ, drive.
Ad · pellŏ (app-), accost.
Com · pellŏ (conp-), drive together.

Ex · pellō, drive out.
Im · pellō (inp-), incite.
Re · pellō, drive back.

1. PAR-, POR-, PER-, through, far, reach, try.
Pār, equal.
Per, through.
Ex · perior, test.
Perīclitor, test.
Perīculum, danger.
Porta, gate.
Portō, bear.
Op · portūnus (obp-), suitable.
Paulis · per, for a short time.

2. PAR-, POR-, part, breed.
Parātus, ready.
Com · parō (conp-), get ready.
Pro · perō, hasten.
Im · perātor (inp-), commander.
Im · perō (inp-), command.
Im · perium (inp-), command.
A · pertus [for ab · partus], open.
Re · periō, find.
Pars, portion.
Partim, partly.
O · portet [for ob · portet], is necessary.

PARC-, PLEC-, bind, weave, fold.
Du · plex, two-fold.
Sup · plex (subp-), suppliant.
Sup · plicātiō (subp-), thanksgiving.

Prope, near [with metathesis of r and change of c to p. Cf. roots SAC and SCAL].

Proximus [~~superl. of propior~~], ~~nearest~~.
Proximē, ~~last~~.
Propinquus, ~~near~~.
Propinquitās, ~~proximity~~.
Ad · propinquō (app-), approach.
Propter, near, ~~on account of~~.
Propter · eā, for the reason (that).

1. PAT-, go.
Passus, ~~step~~.
Pōns, bridge.

2. PAT-, PAD-, spread, open.
Pateō, extend.
Pate · faciō, open.
Pandō, extend.

PAV-, little.
Paucus, few.
Parvulus, slight.
Paulum, a little.
Paulō, a little.
Paululum, very slightly.
Paulātim, gradually.
Paulis · per, for a short time.

PED-, tread.
Pēs, foot.
Pedēs, foot-soldier.
Pedester, of infantry.
Ex · peditus, unemcumbered.
Im · pediō (inp-), hinder.
Im · pedimenta (inp-), baggage.
Op · pidum [for ob-pedum], town.
Op · pidānus (obp-), townsman.

PET-, fly.
Petō, seek.
Im · petus (inp-), charge.

PIS-, crush.
Pīlum [for *pislum*], spear.
Prīmi · pīlus, first centurion of
the *triarii*.

PLAT-, spread, flat.
Latus [for *platus*], side.
Plānitiēs [for *platnitiēs*], plain.

PLE-, PLO-, PLV-, fill.
Com · pleō (conp-), fill.
Plērus · que, the most of.
Plūs, more.
Plūrimum, most.
Com · plūrēs (conp-), many.

Mani · pulus, maniple.
Am · plius, more.
Ampli · ficō, enlarge.
?Pellis, skin.
Populus, people.
Pūblicus [for *populicus*], belong-
ing to the state.

PLV-, PLOV-, wash, flow.
Ex · plōrō [for *ex · ploverō*], recon-
noitre.
Ex · plōrātor, scout.

POS-, behind.
Post, after.
Post · eā, afterwards.
Post · quam, after.
Postrī · diē [for *posterō diē*], next
day.

POT-, master.
Potius, rather.
Pos · sum [for *potis sum*], be able,
can.

Potēns, able.
Potestās, power.
Potior, gain.
Im · petrō (inp-), obtain.

PREC-, pray.
Dē · precor, petition against.
Poscō [for *porcscō*], demand.
Postulō, demand.

PRO-, PRI-, PRAE-, before.
Prō, before.
Prior, preceding.
Prius · quam, sooner than.
Prīs · tinus [for *prius · tinus*], for-
mer.
Prīmus, first.
Prīmum, in the first place.
Prīmō, in the first place.
Prīn · ceps [for *prīmi · ceps*], leader.
Prīmi · pīlus, first centurion of
the *triarii*.
Prae, before.

RA-, join, count.
Ratiō, reason.
Rēs, thing.

RAP-, RVP-, snatch, break.
Dī · ripiō [for *dis · ripiō*], sack.
Ē · ruptiō, sally.
Rūpēs, cliff.

REG-, RIG-, stretch, guide.
Por · rigō [for *prō · regō*], stretch
out.
Regiō, direction.
Rēx, ruler.
Rēgnum, control.

1. SA-, SI-, sow, strow, sift.
Pŏnŏ [for *port· (prō) sinō*], place.
Lᴊ pōnŏ, put off.
Ⲅrŏ·pŏnŏ, display.

2. SA-, SIM-, together, like.
Sĭngŭlĭ, one at a time.
Sĭngŭlārĭs, extraordinary.
Sĭmul, at the same time.
Cŏn·sĭmĭlĭs, altogether like.

3. SA-, pronominal stem.
Sĭ·c [for *si·ce*], so.
I·pse, self.

1. SAC-, SAG-, fasten.
Săgĭttārĭus, archer.
Saepēs [with *p* for *c*], hedge.

2. SAC-, SEC-, SCĪD-, CĪD-, split.
Saxum, rock.
Sectĭŏ, booty.
Scĭentĭa, knowledge.
Inter·scĭndŏ, cut off.
Con·cīdŏ, cut to pieces.
In·cīdŏ, cut into.
Oc·cīdŏ, kill.

3. SAC-, show.
Sĭgnum, signal.
Sĭgnĭ·fer, standard-bearer,
Sĭgnĭ·ficŏ, announce.
Sĭgnĭ·ficātĭŏ, signal.
In·sĭgne, sign.

SAL-, SER-, save.
Salūs, safety.
Sōlus, alone.
Sōlum, only.

Sollĭ·cĭtŏ (sōlĭ), stir up.
Servŏ, keep.
Cŏn·servŏ, preserve.

SCAD-, CAD-, cover.
Castra, camp.
Castellum, redoubt.

SCAL-, SCAR- (with *p* for *c*,
SPOL-), scrape.
Calamĭtās, [for *scalamitās*], dis-
aster.
Dē·spolĭŏ, deprive.
?Populor, Dē·populor, ravage

SCAND-, climb.
A·scendŏ (adsc-), mount.
A·scēnsus (adsc-), ascent.

SCARP-, SCALP-, cut, scratch.
Scrībŏ, write.
Cŏn·scrībŏ, enroll.
Prae·scrībŏ, dictate.

SCV-, CV-, cover, hide.
Scūtum, shield.
Custōdĭa, guard.

SEC-, follow.
Sequor, follow.
Cŏn·sequor, attain.
In·sequor, follow up.
Prō·sequor, pursue.
Sub·sequor, follow closely.
Secundus, favorable.
Secundum, according to.
Con- [for *scom-*], with.
Cum, with.
Cōpĭa [for *com·opia*], supply.

Con·trā, against.
Con·trārius, opposite.

SED-, SID-, sit.
Pos·sideō [for prō·sideo], own.
In·sidiae, stratagem.
Ob·sēs, hostage.
Prae·sidium, garrison.
Sub·sidium, assistance.
Super·sedeō, omit.
Cŏn·sīdŏ, settle.

SEN-, old.
Senātor, elder, senator.
Senātus, senate.

SENT-, feel.
Sententia, opinion.
Cŏn·sentiŏ, agree.
Cŏn·sēnsus, agreement.

1. SER-, SVAR-, string, bind.
Dē·serŏ, abandon.
Prae·sertim, especially.
Servitūs, slavery.

2. SER-, SVAL-, bright.
Sŏl, sun.
Silva, forest.
Silvestris, wooded.

1. SMAR-, MAR-, think.
Mora, delay.
Moror, delay.

Memoria, remembrance.
Com·memorŏ(conm-), mention.

2. SMAR-, MER-, ascribe.
Meritum, merit.
Mercātor, trader.

SOVO-, SVO-, own.
Suī, of himself, etc.
Suus, his, etc.
Cŏn·suēscŏ, be accustomed.
Cŏn·suētūdŏ, custom.
Mān·suētūdŏ, gentleness.

Sed, but.
?Sī, if.
?Sī·ne, without.
?Nī·si, if not.

SPA-, PA-, draw, stretch.
Spatium, space.
Spēs, hope.
Dē·spērŏ, give up hope.

?Studeŏ, strive after.
?Studium, eagerness.

SPEC-, see, spy.
Cŏn·spiciŏ, espy.
Per·spiciŏ, ascertain.
Re·spiciŏ, look back.
Ex·spectŏ, await.
Cŏn·spicor, espy.
Speciēs, form.
Speculātor, spy.
Cŏn·spectus, sight.
Dē·spectus, view downward.
Prŏ·spectus, view forward.

STA-, stand, set.
Cŏn·stanter, uniformly.
In·stŏ, press forward.
Prae·stŏ, excel, show.
Cŏn·sistŏ, take position.
Dē·sistŏ, stop.
In·sistŏ, take a stand.

Re·sistŏ, resist.
Statuŏ, determine.
Cŏn·stituŏ, determine.
Statim, at once.
Statiŏ, picket.
Statūra, stature.

STER-, STRA-, STLA-, strow,
spread.
Lātus [old, stlātus], broad.
Lātitūdŏ, width.

STRV-, spread, heap.
Ex·struŏ, erect.
Īn·struŏ, arrange.

1. TA-, TEN-, stretch.
Prīs·tinus [for prius·tinus], for-
mer.
Prŏ·tinus, at once.
Tener, tender.
Teneŏ, hold.
Con·tineŏ, restrain, keep.
Dis·tineŏ, separate.
Ob·tineŏ, hold.
Per·tineŏ, extend to.
Re·tineŏ, detain.
Sus·tineŏ [for subs·tineŏ], sus-
tain.
Sus·tentŏ [for subs·tentŏ], hold
out.
Tendŏ, stretch.
Con·tendŏ, hasten.
?Tempus, time.

2. TA-, pronominal stem, third
person, demonstrative.
Tam, so.
Tantus, so great.

Tantulus, so trifling.
Tamen, still.
Tot·idem, just as many.
Tum, then.
    Also the final element in au·tem
    au·t, i·ta, i·ta·que, u·t.

TAG-, touch, seize.
At·tingŏ (adt-), touch.
Red·in·tegrŏ, renew.

TARC- (TARP-), TREP-, turn,
twist.
Tormentum, engine for hurling.
Turpitūdŏ, disgrace.
Trabs, beam.

TEC-, TAX-, weave, arrange.
In·texŏ, weave in.
Tēlum (for teclum), spear.

TEM-, TAN-, cut.
Con·temptus, contempt.
Con·tumēlia, insult.

TER-, TREM-, TERS-, shake,
scare.
Dē·terreŏ, prevent.
Per·terreŏ, thoroughly frighten.
Terror, fright.

TV-, TVM-, TAV-, TO-, swell.
Tumulus, mound.
Tumultus, uproar.
Tōtus, whole.

TVR-, harry, crowd.
Per·turbŏ, throw into confusion.
Prŏ·turbŏ, drive off.
?Turris, tower.

VAG-, VEH-, move, carry.
**Vĕxillum**, flag.
**Vĕxŏ**, harass.

1. VEL-, VAL-, VER-, cover, guard.
**Vāllum**, rampart.
**Inter · vāllum**, distance.
**Vereor**, fear.

2. VEL-, VOL-, tear, pluck.
**Vulnus**, wound.
**Vulnerŏ**, wound.

VER-, say.
**Verbum**, word.
**Vērŏ**, in truth.

VERG-, VRG-, VALG-, slope, press.
**Vergŏ**, incline.
**Urgeŏ**, press.
**Vulgŏ (volgŏ)**, generally.

VERT-, turn.
**Ā · vertŏ**, turn away.
**Con · vertŏ**, turn around.
**Re · vertŏ**, return.
**Re · vertor**, return.
**Versŏ**, turn about, *pass.* dwell.
**Ad · versus**, opposite.
**Dī · versus**, turned away.
**Intr · ŏrsus** [for *intrŏ · versus*], within.
**R · ûrsus** [for *re · vorsus*], again.
**Trāns · versus**, at right-angles.
**Ūni · versus**, all.

VET-, VIT-, year, old.
**In · veterāscŏ**, grow old in.
**Vetŏ**, forbid.

VI-, VIC-, twine.
**Vīnea**, covered shed.
**Vīnum**, wine.
**Vīmen**, willow, withe.

VIC-, conquer.
**Vincŏ**, conquer.
**Vīctor**, victorious.
**Prŏ · vincia**, province.
**Vīx**, barely.

VID-, see.
**Videŏ**, see.
**In · videŏ**, envy.
**Prŏ · videŏ**, procure.
**Prū · dentia** [for *prŏ · videntia*], wisdom.
**Im · prŏ · vīsŏ (inp-)**, unexpectedly.

VIR-, man.
**Vīr**, man.
**Vīrtūs**, valor.

VOC-, VAG-, call.
**Con · vocŏ**, call together.
**Re · vocŏ**, call back.
**Vŏx**, voice.

VOL-, will, wish.
**Voluntās**, wish.
**N · ŏlŏ** [for *nē · vŏlō*], be unwilling.
**Quam · vīs**, howsoever.

————

**At**, but.

{ **At·que**, and.
  **Āc**,

**Et**, and.
**Et·iam**, even.
**Ad**, to.
**Ap·ud**, among.

**Ex**, **Ē**, from, out of.
**Extrēmus**, furthest.

**Locus** [for *stlocus*], place.
**Con·locō** (coll-), place.

**Multus**, much.
**Multitūdō**, large number.

**Proelium**, battle.
**Proelior**, fight.

**Superior**, higher.
**Summus** [for *supimus*], highest.
**Suprā**, above.
**Superō**, overcome.

**Tardus**, slow.
**Tardō**, retard.

**Trēs**, three.
**Trī·duum**, three days' time.
**Tribūnus**, military tribune.
**Tertius**, third.

16380388R00085

Printed in Great Britain
by Amazon